AURA

Shield of Protection & Glory

T.S.G. PUBLISHING FOUNDATION, INC.

TORKOM
SARAYDARIAN

The Aura

ISBN: 0-929874-06-4

Library of Congress Catalog Card Number: 92-90922

Printed in the United States of America

Cover Design:	*A Design Studio* Sedona, Arizona
Printed by:	*Data Reproductions* Rochester Hills, Michigan
Published by:	T.S.G. Publishing Foundation, Inc. Post Office Box 7068 Cave Creek, Arizona 85327-7068 United States of America

Note: Meditations, visualizations, and other health information are given as guidelines. They should be used with discretion and after receiving professional advice.

Table of Contents

Charts

"It must be mentioned here that the aura is not the etheric body. The aura is the radiation of the physical, emotional and mental bodies, and, if a person is advanced, the aura also has strong radiations of the soul and Intuitional, Atmic, Monadic, and Divine energies. All these forces and energies form a field around the physical body. The aura has many colors, continuous fluctuations, and an egg-shaped form. Any thought, emotion, or action changes the colors and waves of the aura."

"The aura also should not be confused with the halo seen around the heads of Great Ones. That also is composed of the radiations of the head center. It expands beyond the head and forms a multicolored sphere. Sometimes the halo is the twelve-petaled Lotus on the higher mental plane; sometimes it is the vehicle of a great Spirit overshadowing the person."

– New Dimensions in Healing, p. 48

"We sometimes hear the term 'health aura.' The health aura is prana which circulates through a person's etheric body and radiates out. This surface radiation is called the health aura. It is a golden hue, and if it is clear and even over all parts of the body, the health of the body is perfect. But if it loses its radiance and fades away, or in certain parts totally disappears or mixes with grey colors, that location is not healthy and needs immediate attention."

– New Dimensions in Healing, p. 70

Published from donations to the
Torkom Saraydarian Book Publishing Fund

Chapter 1

The Aura

The aura is a very sensitive envelope or sphere around the body. Almost everything that happens in the Universe affects the aura, but the brain cannot register the effect until the etheric brain is developed and engaged with the physical brain to translate the impressions and pass them to the physical brain.

An average person's aura is mostly composed of the etheric body and the emotional body, with very few patches of the mental body. After the first initiation, the mental body increases in the aura. Later, intuitional and higher radiations come into the aura, making it a rainbow of many translucent colors.

The average person has his physical body, plus his etheric double with its centers and etheric counterparts of the physical organs. Not all of the etheric centers are active. Usually the sex center, the solar plexus, and to some degree the throat center, show signs of activity.

The average person's astral body is a chaotic mist in the aura. All astral centers are dormant, except those which correspond to the active etheric centers.

The average person's mental body is an unorganized, diffused cloud around the head and shoulders. The sacral center in the mental body appears active; other vehicles do not yet exist. This is why the aura of an average person cannot register spatial impressions.

People have the opinion that they have an astral body. The fact is that few people have a well-organized, well-developed, and unfolded astral body. They do have an astral emanation, which is congested with hatred, fear, jealousy, various glamors, greed, and anger. This kind of astral aura is similar to a stagnant pool, where the germs of many destructive physical and social diseases multiply.

The astral and mental auras originate from the corresponding permanent atoms. Permanent atoms ooze out a vapor-like substance which builds the astral and mental bodies. The aura of the bodies begins to form when the bodies interact with the corresponding environment. If the human soul controls such an interaction and makes it more conscious and goal fitting, the aura expands. The expansion of the aura depends upon

> — the conscious use of the corresponding body
> — the virtues nourished in that body
> — the service rendered by that body

The astral body and the astral aura need conscious striving and scientific procedures to be built properly, in order to be used as a communication tool with the astral world.

How do we build our aura? First comes sincere aspiration toward higher values; then worship and admiration of great beauty; then intense devotion to spiritual principles and dedication to the service of humanity. These are methods by which one can purify his astral aura and make it radioactive and beautiful. It is in this stage that the centers and senses in the astral body emerge, develop, and begin to function. Unless the centers and senses work in the astral body, one does not have an astral vehicle. Instead, there are only a lot of glamors and negative emotions around the body.

Some psychics who are clairvoyant attempt to read the auras of others. This is a very dangerous practice because an average psychic is mostly focused in his astral body and looks at the auras of others through his own colorful window full of maya, glamors, and negative emotions. Such psychics are very poor guides who often disappear in the crucial moments of your life.

Many people do not have a mental aura because they do not have a developed mind. Everyone of us must build his mental body and his mental aura, just as we build our physical body.

When the mental body is in the process of formation, it radiates a yellow mist into the aura, especially around the head. When the astral body is in formation, it radiates silvery blue mist into the aura. The etheric body radiates golden and violet colors into the aura. The etheric aura is violet, but in the coils of the etheric body travel prana, which appears golden. Golden light circulates in the etheric body, if it is healthy.

Wherever the golden aura turns brown or black, there is a point of trouble in the body. The etheric body is built by hard labor, swimming, running, climbing mountains, eating good food, and using lots of fresh water.

The mental body is built through concentration, meditation, visualization, and contemplation. As the mental body forms and develops, yellow rays can be seen emanating from the head and melting gradually into the aura.

As the human aura builds up and higher ethers form into bodies, the contact of the person with the Universe expands, and eventually the aura becomes a mirror which reflects all that transpires in the seven planes of the Cosmic Physical Plane.

The aura in its totality is a sense organ. It is a collective sense which allows the human soul to communicate with the forces of the environment, the forces of the etheric, astral, mental, and higher realms. The aura is also a vehicle by which one can travel on land, on the astral plane, on the mental plane, and, when it is highly organized, on higher planes. Following are important tabulations:

Colors of the Etheric Centers

Center	# of Petals	Color
Head	12 petals	white and gold
Ajna	96 petals	rose, yellow, blue, purple
Throat	16 petals	purple, silver
Heart	12 petals	golden
Solar Plexus	10 petals	rose mixed with green
Sacral	6 petals	orange, vermillion
Base of Spine	4 petals	red, orange

Etheric Centers, Rays, and Kingdoms

Center	Ray	Kingdom
Head	1	Solar lives
Ajna	2	Planetary lives
Throat	3	Kingdom of souls
Heart	4	Vegetable kingdom
Solar Plexus	6	Animal kingdom
Sacral	5	Humanity
Base of Spine	7	Mineral kingdom

Sound and Colors

Note of the Scale	Color
C	Red
D	Orange
E	Yellow
F	Yellow-green
G	Blue-green
A	Blue-violet
B	Red-violet

Rays and Colors

Ray	Color
1	Red
2	Blue
3	Yellow
4	Orange
5	Green
6	Violet
7	Indigo

Seven Bodies and Colors

Body	Color
Etheric/physical	Violet-green
Emotional	Silver-blue
Mental	Yellow-green
Intuitional	Midnight blue
Atmic	Orange
Monadic	Indigo, yellow-orange
Divine	Crimson red, orange, ruby

Color Combinations

Color	Combination	Resulting Color
Red	(Yellow + Blue)	Green
Yellow	(Red + Blue)	Violet
Blue	(Red + Yellow)	Orange

Colors and Corresponding Elements

Color	Effect	Element
Red	Arterial stimulant	Ammonia
Orange	Continuous builder	Carbonate, lime
Yellow	Cathartic	Calomel * *(a compound of chlorine and mercury)
Yellow-green	Cleanser	Sulphur
Green	Disinfectant	Chlorides
Blue-green	Absorbent	Boric acid
Blue	Alleviator of pain	Citric acid
Indigo	Astringent	Aconitum
Violet	Motor nerve depressant	Opium
Yellow-violet	Digestant	Chloral hydrate
Violet-red	Emotional stabilizer	Digitalis (foxglove)
Blue-red	Cardiac energizer	Potassium nitrate

States of the Aura

Mobilization of the aura starts in puberty, or during the first menstrual period. The first intercourse may leave a permanent rhythm and influence in the aura. This is one reason why virginity was strictly observed until the right person was found.

Mobilization also occurs

    a. with childbirth

    b. during the moment of a solemn oath or decision

    c. at the time of initiation, when the aura changes

    d. when contact is made with an advanced Teacher

    e. at the moment of aesthetic ecstasy

    f. during moments of true love, without physical love

Auras fuse in a certain way during kissing and in intercourse if contraceptives are not used. There are two places which are open for mixing the aura: the mouth and the sex organs, when orgasm is simultaneous.

Full moons are times when the coloring of the entire aura changes. A person's "true colors" can only be observed during the full moon of his rising sign. Each constellation has its key color which, when absorbed, changes the entire aura, mixing with its original colors and forming combinations of colors. This process is called the chemistry of colors, which is related to the Ray of the sign and of the person.

Constellations and Aura

Constellation	Virtue	Color	Note
Aries	Striving	Red	C
Taurus	Gratitude	Red-orange	C#
Gemini	Harmlessness	Orange	D
Cancer	Discrimination	Yellow-orange	D#
Leo	Courage	Yellow	E
Virgo	Solemnity	Yellow-green	F
Libra	Responsibility	Green	F#
Scorpio	Fearlessness	Blue-green	G
Sagittarius	Patience	Blue	G#
Capricorn	Daring	Blue-violet	A
Aquarius	Compassion	Violet	A#
Pisces	Service	Red-violet	B

Size of the Aura

The larger and more proportionate the aura is to the body, the healthier the person is. An aura which is narrow and irregular in proportion to the body means there are problems in the body, emotions, or mind.

When the physical body is sick, the aura does not radiate regularly. The aura is narrower around the parts of the body that are sick.

It is similar for the subtle bodies. Each subtle body shrinks toward the physical body, as a dry fruit shrinks and loses its color.

A healthy person radiates a seven to nine foot aura, with clear colors. Radiation of the aura extends further when one dresses in white. The colors of the aura indicate changes in the state of consciousness, the voltage and intensity of thoughts, the density of emotions, and the pressure of actions. The pressure of actions originates from the intentions and motives behind them. All our thoughts, emotions, and actions create changes in the colors of our aura.

Changes in the aura can be seen

1. when new inspirations and impressions reach the aura
2. during exposure to violent emotions or violent group activities
3. during travel from place to place, where different colors predominate
4. when we change the level of our consciousness from plane to plane
5. when we contact an Initiate or Higher Being, or contact planetary and solar centers
6. during magnetic or electrical storms
7. when we relate with the opposite sex

The colors of the aura must be evaluated through the following:

— their luminosity
— their purity
— their depth
— the way they blend
— their stability

— the way they return to their original color
   after a sudden change

— their size

Pale, muddy colors; colors without depth; colors with sharp edges; unstable, narrow, and rigid colors all are signs of an unhealthy aura.

Each color in the aura is a tuning key with the corresponding plane. One can enter into the plane consciously if the color is clear, pure, and dense.

Protective colors are formed by our

- love
- gratitude
- solemnity
- nobility
- honesty
- enthusiasm
- lofty thoughts and emotions
- abstinence

Love refers to a love that is active and expresses itself in action to help people go forward on the path of their evolution. To love means to free yourself gradually from selfishness, separatism, greed, luxury, and vanity and try to live, feel, and think for the benefit of other people. Such a love brings beautiful colors into the aura from the love petals of the Chalice. Love currents have great power of healing.

Gratitude also channels energy from the Chalice to the aura. In a spirit of gratitude, the atomic substance increases in the aura and makes it magnetic. Atomic substance is built by the atoms of the highest levels of each plane.

Solemnity makes the aura a royal beauty. The aura of a solemn person is charged with deep royal blue and crimson red. Solemnity brings energy from the higher petals of the Chalice and makes the aura powerful, influential. It inspires trust, power, and magnanimity. Solemnity creates a continuous flow of psychic energy into the aura.

Nobility is the state of a person who stands in close contact with his Master, or with the Hierarchy. Noble people have extraordinarily beautiful rainbow auras. Invisible beings respect and love noble people, and often come to visit them, giving them love and respect.

Honesty creates harmony and rhythm in the aura. Any dishonest act disturbs the stability and rhythmic circulation of the aura. Honesty orchestrates the colors and movements in the aura, and with each honest act the colors become more pure and real. Honesty awakens sleeping values and virtues in other people.

Enthusiasm charges the aura with electrical fire, which spreads to those who come in contact with such a person. Enthusiasm creates sublimation in the aura. In each body, the lower atoms travel to the higher levels and radiate their purest colors. The fire of enthusiasm is the furnace of transmutation in the aura.

Lofty thoughts and emotions nourish the aura, repair, and protect it. With every lofty thought, our aura contacts higher reservoirs of energy in space. As rivers and streams serve a lake, so do good thoughts and emotions feed the aura.

Abstinence also has an effect on the aura. When the sexual force is sublimated, it increases the strength and beauty of the aura. Sexual energy is creative. When sublimated, it first becomes part of the etheric body, then becomes part of the astral and mental bodies.

Sexual energy makes the aura highly charged and magnetic. Healing energy increases in the aura if one abstains for a long time. Actually, our thoughts and emotions are the children of our sublimated sexual energy. Mental fire is a higher correspondence of sexual energy. This creative energy travels all the way to the Chalice and accumulates in certain petals.

A beautiful poem, painting, or other work of art is sublimated sexual energy, molded by a vision. Sexual energy increases in the aura when two people love each other greatly, but abstain from sex for a while. The two auras begin to interchange energy, and thus the love energy between them deepens and sublimation takes place. In addition to this, one feels balance, stability, and equilibrium in his nature, and he conducts his life with wisdom and grace.

Each color in the aura is a sound. Because of a specific color in your aura, you may tend to use a certain note in the sounds you make or in your speech. That color either controls all other colors and becomes your dominating key, or you were hypnotized by certain sounds and that note is forced upon your aura, increasing the corresponding color or substance in your aura. In both cases, by using the same note repeatedly, one may create total imbalance in his auric system and hurt the centers and organs related to that note.

The same problems occur if a person is continuously exposed to the same color. This is why we see large paintings or tapestries of rainbow colors in some esoteric schools.

In studying the note which a person uses in his conversation, one can easily discover which of his bodies is stimulated, and what kind of troubles can be expected in the future.

Singing is considered a healthy sign. When birds or people are sick, they do not sing. Singing is proof that the aura is balanced and that the person is not caught in a groove but can go from one color (note) to another, stimulating or revitalizing many of them. When a person stops singing, you see that his aura is not healthy; it has an imbalance of colors and many other complications.

Music is very closely connected to our health. Certain nations have national sicknesses which are caused by the music that the people of that nation constantly hear. Some groups develop heart, liver, and kidney problems because of the kind of music they hear. It is impossible to indicate which music is good or bad for an individual, but in general, any loud music, rock-and-roll, acid rock, disco, or similar music stimulates the kidneys, solar plexus, and sacral center. The diseases contracted by people who listen to these kinds of music originate from these sources.

Music can retard or assist the development of the aura. Certain notes affect the etheric and physical bodies. Certain notes affect the astral and mental bodies. Music that makes an advanced person greatly disturbed may suit the emotions of an average person and give him great pleasure. Some people, not having an organized mental aura, do not respond to those notes, so they are safe. Those who have a mental aura, however, become highly disturbed.

Beautiful and creative music harmonizes and balances the aura of the listener, purifies, and energizes it. Such music is usually composed by an artist who has the same purity, energy, and balance.

One creates out of his true being. Disturbing music creates imbalance in the aura, increasing dramatically certain colors, and greatly reducing the colors of the higher vehicles.

Chapter 2

The Aura as a
Mechanism of Contact

The aura has geometrical formations in it. Lines of light and lines of fiery colors form many geometrical formations, extending from one center to another, from one plane to another. If these formations are harmonious and tend to appear as triangles or circles, we say that the human soul is advanced and radioactive.

The geometrical formations start from the etheric centers. They then extend toward the astral and mental centers. Next, the geometrical lines focus themselves in the Chalice. One can see streams of energy flowing back and forth from the centers to the Chalice, and then from the Chalice to the centers.

The aura consists of eight kinds of substance:

1. physical substance
2. etheric substance

3. astral substance

4. mental substance

5. Intuitional substance

6. Atmic substance

7. Monadic substance

8. Divine substance

Intuitional, Atmic, Monadic and Divine substances are substances of the higher or Cosmic ethers.

All eight kinds of substance exist in the aura, in greater or lesser quantities. As a person advances spiritually, the substances found in the various vehicles come into greater balance and harmony. Various substances are more evenly distributed in the aura, and the colors are perfectly orchestrated into a symphony within the aura. Such an orchestration brings a person greater beauty, health, sanity, strength, and creativity.

When the eight kinds of substance are highly organized with their specific centers and senses, they work as a mechanism of contact with similar substances throughout the Universe. For example, we have radiations that are chemical, etheric, astral, and mental. We also have radiations which are ideas, directions, inspirations, and impressions. The eight spheres within the aura slowly become sensitive to these radiations, and they record and register them, assimilate, and then release them through their activities. Thus, these eight spheres bring the human soul in contact with the greater Universe.

The first sphere is the *physical aura*. It is related to chemical radiations. These radiations come from rocks, minerals, metals, precious stones, wood, and so on. These radiations can be constructive or destructive to the aura; in most cases, a healthy physical aura balances its reception and repels those radiations which are not beneficial to its nature.

Physical radiations are picked up through the skin and hair. The physical aura absorbs some of them, breaks their voltage, assimilates them for nourishment, and then rejects the rest. If the physical aura is not healthy, radiations from the dense world can penetrate into the physical body and create disturbances within the glands, bloodstream, lymphatic, and nervous systems. If the physical aura is healthy, it exercises an automatic control over the radiations and does not permit entry to any dangerous ones.

It is even possible to reject atomic radiation by strengthening the physical aura through certain exercises and chemicals. For example, we see that not everyone who works close to places where there is radioactivity reacts in the same way. Some people are heavily affected; some resist contamination for a long time. Resistance is the result of the health of our physical aura.

The second sphere, the *etheric aura*, registers etheric radiations and puts us in contact with the etheric sphere of the planet. The etheric aura registers the radiations from the etheric centers of people and from the chakras of cities, mountains, and nations.

For example, New York is the throat center of the world; Washington, D.C. is the head center of the United States; Los Angeles is the heart center of the United States. Cities, mountains, and large bodies of water have their own centers, which are registered by our etheric body. These are registered not only as radiations, but as states of consciousness and beingness.

If the etheric body is really healthy, it is able to register the condition of the chakras found all over the world. It is important to know that the condition of these chakras in the etheric sphere reflect the coming world conditions. For example, you can feel with your heart chakra all those energies which will create changes on the planet; you can feel the heart pulse of coming events. With your head center, you can register the plans that are being formed in the minds of people. With your solar plexus chakra, you register the emotional situations in the world. With a developed etheric aura, you can sense things going on in the chakras of nations and cities.

Wherever you are, through your etheric aura you are in contact with major or minor chakras. If your etheric aura is healthy, it balances the incoming and outflowing energies. If it is not balanced, the incoming energies create confusion, disturbance, and unhealthy conditions in the etheric body, which in due time reflect on your physical body.

Etheric radiations not only interchange through chakras but also through touch and physical contact, such as a handshake, kiss, or intercourse. The hands, lips, and generative organs are surrounded with active etheric centers; through these centers, etheric auras usually fuse within each other, for good or for bad.

The third sphere, the *emotional aura*, has its centers and senses as well. It has a very powerful influence over the whole aura. Any violent emotion can spread its color throughout the aura, and sometimes the waves of the emotional aura can be seen covering all other colors and motions in the aura for a long time. This, of course, damages the constitution of the entire aura in varying degrees.

The astral aura absorbs or registers the emotions of people. In extreme cases, it absorbs so much that the person has a hard time controlling himself. The emotional aura may register the astral radiations coming from entities living in the astral plane. Those who pass away still have their emotions, and if a person is keyed in with these centers in any way, he receives their emotions. Most of these receptions are unconscious, but they still affect our life heavily, leading us from joy and happiness to depression, inertia, and gloom.

If one is attached to people who have passed away, such as a father, mother, child, husband, wife, or lover, he especially absorbs their emotions and feels various changing moods in his daily life. Many children who have died continuously send astral messages to their mothers and their mothers continuously receive these messages and live in them. Such astral emotions are dense within the sphere of the world, especially during times of war when thousands of people die in extremely emotional states.

We also absorb the emanations of emotional clouds through our astral aura. These emotional clouds are formed by the massive emotional outbursts of big crowds. There are good and bad clouds; some are charged with joy, happiness, aspiration, and ecstasy, while others are charged with hatred, revenge, and fear. People commonly contact such cloud formations.

If the emotional cloud is charged with joy, happiness, and ecstasy, it becomes a source of blessing for the world. Sometimes the kind of pollution accumulated in the dark clouds is more costly for our health and happiness than physical pollution. Such clouds carry special kinds of acid and other destructive precipitations all over the globe, disturbing and destroying life everywhere.

Emotional clouds are sometimes so thick that one can almost touch them. Clouds of anger, fear, and revenge send heavy emanations to people; they feel the overcasting gloom which is going to precipitate in their lives. It is noticed that animals can feel the emanations of such clouds.

Emotional clouds sometimes last a long time and condition the lives of millions of people. Epidemics and natural catastrophes are often the direct result of such accumulations. The dark accumulations of emotional clouds result in various sicknesses, mostly affecting the liver, spleen, pancreas, and other systems in the body.

If the astral aura is highly sensitive, it can come in contact with the Cosmic Astral Plane. Such a contact may be very destructive to the person, if he is not shielded by the power of Spirit. Also, certain black magicians, who are embodiments of crime or evil, come in contact with the dark forces found on the Cosmic Astral Plane and become a channel between those forces and earth. Such people bring revenge, war, destruction, and widespread moral degeneration. It must be remembered that these forces can contact our astral aura if there are grave accumulations within our aura.

The fourth sphere, the *mental aura*, puts us in contact with the mental world. The mental aura is a lemon-yellow sphere around our head and shoulders which attracts the thoughts of people. Through this aura, one becomes aware of the thoughts of other people.

People can read the thoughts of others if the mental aura is highly organized. The mental aura is not easily visible, but it is there like the magnetic field of a magnet. It is true that things which we cannot see control our life more than that which we can see. One cannot see the mind, various emotions, or even the True Self, but these run the show of a person's life. What we see is an effect of what we cannot see.

Sometimes the mental aura is extremely sensitive and absorbs the thoughts of others like a sponge. The mental aura can also register the thoughts of departed ones from the mental plane. Great writers, artists, and scientists especially like to project their thoughts to the thought-world of human beings. Their thoughts surround us, but we lack the capacity to discriminate, choose, or even be aware of them.

This is not a condition of mediumistic contact or channeling, but direct contact through the mental aura of people with those thoughts projected to space, or projected specifically to certain people.

There is an unconscious, but steady, mental conversation being carried on between those who have passed away and those who are living. When the mental aura is highly organized, it becomes possible to find the source of a particular thought and understand motives and the message contained in that thought.

Invisible spirits very often guide and protect their friends during certain occasions through thought. In the same way, those who died in revenge and hatred can still influence people through their emanations. Insanity continues after death and creates widespread disturbances in the world of thought, unless it is insanity caused by brain damage.

Most advanced minds who pass away do not try to exercise any mental control over people; rather, they try to inspire others with beauty, goodness, and wisdom.

We come in contact through our mental sphere with accumulative thought clouds in space. There are many kinds of accumulations ranging from light to deepest darkness, crime, and terror. There are accumulations of beauty, goodness, and wisdom as well as accumulations of terror, crime, and destruction. One can tune in with such accumulations according to how his mental aura is built. Refined and evolved auras naturally repel all lower strata of thought formations and tune in with higher clouds of wisdom and beauty.

If the mental aura is healthy and has a high frequency, it contacts only those thought accumulations which are high-quality, lofty, inclusive, joyful, and creative. But if the mental aura is unhealthy and polluted with various low-level thoughtforms, it becomes a channel for criminal thought and increases the suffering in the world.

When the mental aura is developed and healthy, one can also contact spatial thoughts. These are thoughts released by great Beings, Masters, Initiates, and Leaders, as well as thoughts of angelic beings who work between planet and planet, between solar systems, and between galaxies. Spatial thoughts also include ashramic thoughts on various levels.

People with pure and developed mental auras can contact spatial thoughts, which enrich their lives and make them creative leaders of humanity.

The fifth sphere, that of the *Intuitional aura*, is also called the aura of the Fourth Cosmic Ether. Through the Intuitional aura, one can contact ideas, receive them, and use them creatively. Ideas are electrical in nature. They are waves charged with the Hierarchical Plan, the totality of which is the Plan. Ideas are fragments of the Plan which fit special conditions and levels and prepare the way for the fulfillment of the Plan. Through our Intuitional aura we come in contact with those ideas which move evolution forward.

Great creative people usually have very organized Intuitional auras through which they can transmit the ideas of the New Era. Sometimes their creativity is centuries ahead of their contemporaries, and their expressions lead people toward a greater future. The ideas of highly creative people focus on the Divine Plan for humanity. All their thoughts and creativity are oriented to make this planet a planet of beauty, joy, health, and transformation.

Through the Intuitional aura, one also comes in contact with archetypal ideas, which are projected from the mind of the Great Architect of the Universe. Every form in Nature has its prototypal idea. Geniuses are those who can contact the layers of prototypes and Archetypes.

The sixth sphere, the *Atmic aura*, is also called the aura of the Third Cosmic Ether. Through this aura we come in contact with Cosmic direction. First we receive direction from our innermost Self. Directions are rays of energy which lead you toward the heart of the Cosmos, or toward the Central Cosmic Magnet. Directions also come to us from the "center where the Will of God is known," from the Sun itself, or from other higher Cosmic centers.

We must remember that all existence is directed by powerful forces. The True Self directs your life on the magnetic line which connects you with the heart of the Cosmos. The direction from the "Father's Home" leads your national life. Direction coming from zodiacal signs leads your global life. Direction from higher sources leads your solar life. You can tune in with such directions if your Atmic aura is fully developed.

The seventh sphere, the *Monadic aura,* is also called the Second Cosmic Ether. We are told that the Monadic aura is very sensitive to Cosmic inspirations coming from the seven Rays, galaxies, Cosmic Avatars, and zodiacal sources. Inspiration is a current of energy which brings you a vision or image of prototypes existing on higher planes that carry an image of future perfection to you.

The eighth sphere of the First Cosmic Ether is the *Divine aura.* With the aura of our divine body, we receive impressions from the Greater Zodiac, which is formed by one thousand constellations. The Greater Zodiac is a huge Life which ensouls billions of stars.

Impressions are electrical lines which connect you with the vision of Infinity and impart to you fragments of those plans which are related to the Cosmic Whole. When we contact such impressions, we develop total selflessness. We live in a state of Infinity and gradually fuse with the One Self.

Mankind is the supreme creation of Nature; within the human being lie all possibilities to become aware of all that is. Our communications are unconscious or semiconscious at first, but as we unfold, the True Self spreads a sensitive network of light throughout the whole aura and registers all that is going on in the Universe through the totality of the aura.

How can we develop our aura? There are many methods, but the most supreme technique or method is that of becoming oneself, of becoming the True Self. This process has seven steps:

1. purification
2. striving toward the highest
3. living a sacrificial life
4. living in beauty
5. increasing joy
6. living in freedom
7. meditation

Try to purify your personality vehicles and your environment. Strive toward the highest every day. Try to climb the ladder of evolution. Sacrifice. Meet the real needs of people without expectation. Surround yourself with beauty. Speak beautifully, think beautifully, dream beautifully, and hold people in beauty. As much as possible, increase your joy. Keep your inner joy radiating out. Stand on the firm foundation that Light, Love, and Beauty will conquer. Be joyful as much as possible. Think freely. Speak freely. Do not try to take away the freedom of others. Live in freedom. Daily think about the wisdom of the Teaching. Try to contact higher thoughts and ideas. Try to answer the questions of life through meditation.

When you seriously work on these seven points, your aura will unfold, improve, and form a Robe of Glory around you — and you will become a citizen of the Cosmos.

Chapter 3

The Aura and Healing

The human aura is formed of twelve colors. These colors are the emanations of the

- Etheric body .... gold-violet

- Physical body .... mostly green

- Emotional body .... silvery-blue, plus those colors projected by various emotions

- Lower mental body .... red-yellow, or green

- Higher mental body .... lemon yellow

- Chalice .... orange, rose, yellow

- Solar Angel .... blue-violet

- Intuitional body .... pure blue

- Atmic (Nirvanic) body ...... red-orange

- Monadic body .... yellow-orange,
  indigo

- Divine body .... orange, ruby,
  crimson red

- Self .... pure white

In the Fourth Initiation, the Chalice is dissipated, but Its place is taken by the Spiritual Triad, which carries the original three colors of the Chalice:

- orange
- rose
- yellow

In ancient times, people used to dress according to their rank, level in society, duty, or responsibility. Their mode of dress was an outer manifestation of their state of consciousness and office. Actually, when the "seeing eye" lost its power and the aura began to lose its splendor, people began to dress themselves to create an identity and try to imitate their lost aura.

In those times there were four fundamental divisions, called *castes*. There were laborers, merchants, priests, and the leaders: warriors, or nobles, each dressing differently. People recognized their rank or caste according to the dress, cloth, or uniform in which they were dressed. This was arranged esoterically, depending upon the colors in their aura. The robe or dress of each caste was the externalized symbol of the aura they generally had. As clothing is to the outside world, the aura is to the subjective world. A person is recognized in the subjective world according to his aura.

The aura can be divided into four categories. These four categories are not taken from the field in which a person works, but from the kind of aura a person has. It is possible for an advanced man to work as a laborer; this does not mean that he loses his developed aura.

1. **The aura of an average person** has three dominating colors for the physical, etheric, and emotional bodies. His aura extends from one to three feet. The colors are pale green, pale yellow, and silvery-blue mixed with grey. This is the aura of the laborer, in general.

2. **The aura of the merchant** has three additional colors, and the size of this aura extends from three to six feet. This class consists of those who are esoterically considered to be aspirants. An aspirant is a person who sees the possibility of spiritual development and strives toward it. His striving is mostly related to the physical and emotional body. The dominating colors in his aura are blue, green, orange, yellow, violet, and the colors found in the aura of the laborer.

3. **The next class is called the religious caste, or disciples.** Their aura extends from six to nine feet, and in addition to the previous colors we see red-violet, red, and true orange-yellow. Disciples are those who are dedi-

cated to the manifestation of the Divine Plan in any field of human endeavor.

4. **The fourth group is the caste composed of warriors or nobles.** In esoteric terminology, a member of this caste is a leader, or the Master. His aura extends from nine to thirty feet, as a powerful electromagnetic field of great beauty. The predominant colors, in addition to the ones developed by the previous castes, are indigo, gold, and lemon-red. Masters or nobles have twelve colors as a circular rainbow around their densest vehicle, whatever that vehicle is.

The aura is formed by the emanations radiated out of your vehicles. According to their vibration and frequency, certain colors come into existence. The etheric body is not the aura, but part of it. The health aura is the emanation of the dense physical body. The aura is the totality of all twelve components. These twelve components are not active in low levels of consciousness but come into activity as the real inner Self gains more control over Its vehicles.

The aura of an average person is composed of the radiation of his etheric, physical, astral, and lower mental bodies. As we advance, we build higher bodies and add new substances and colors into our aura. We unfold our centers and they bring greater abundance into our aura.

We have seven centers in our etheric and astral bodies, and four centers in our mental body. These centers add color to the aura as their motions become three or four dimensional, as follows:

1. The head center radiates white-gold as its predominant keynote within the symphony of twelve colors.

2. The center between the brows has ninety-six petals within two large white petals; one-half radiates rose-yellow, and the other half radiates blue-purple.

3. The throat center has sixteen petals, which are purple and blue-violet.

4. The heart center has twelve petals which emanate brilliant orange, vermillion, and gold. As it opens, the gold increases on the petals and mixes with an electrical blue mist.

5. The solar plexus center radiates blue-green through its ten petals. Blue is related to the higher part of the solar plexus; green is related to the lower part.

6. The sacral center has six petals of brilliant orange fire.

7. The base of spine center has four petals, which are crimson red.

We have seven similar centers in the astral body. In the mental body, however, we have centers which correspond to the base of spine center, sacral center, solar plexus, and spleen, which emanate their individual colors into the yellow mental aura.

Thus we see that as a person develops, unfolds, and approaches spiritual perfection, his aura demonstrates a symphony of color, scintillating within twelve predominating colors. A person is thus recognized subjectively by his aura, just as if it were his uniform.

For example, when one enters the emotional plane, he is recognized by the external clarity and beauty of his aura. If his aura is pale or contaminated with various negative emotions, if it is unstable and ugly, he can only remain in the lower levels of the astral plane; no admittance is given to him to enter the higher astral plane so that he can contact higher forces or advanced souls in that plane. Imagine what would happen to a man who attended a wedding ceremony with ragged clothes which smelled heavily of bad odors.

We enter the subjective planes according to the body that we build. For example, if we have a physical body, we can function on the physical plane. With the etheric body we can function on the etheric plane. With the astral body, we can function in the astral plane, and with the mental body, we can function in the mental plane, and so on.

If by chance one enters a higher plane without having the corresponding vehicle, he is electrically evicted; he awakens sharply, or receives a strong shock. An average person only enters the etheric plane, or travels as far as the lowest levels of the astral plane. Aspirants enter the astral plane and can penetrate into the lower mental plane. Disciples can enter the higher mental plane and can occasionally reach the lower levels of the Intuitional Plane. Initiates of high degree or Masters function in the Intuitional Plane and penetrate into higher planes, according to Their rank.

One who walks in the halls of the Intuitional Plane is dressed like a rainbow. Higher bodies are glorious bodies which radiate joy, blessings, and healing energies. These bodies are built throughout the ages through conscious labor. Their radiations come into being as our virtues control our daily life, our words, and thoughts. Actually, the aura is a flow of virtues. Each virtue has its own color, according to its purity and maturity. As the virtue flows from the Core of our being, the radiation of beauty increases in our aura.

The higher the body you have, the more you are in contact with Higher Worlds, where the Plan is prepared, where the secret purpose of all creation exists. As you go higher, you become more aware of the greater mysteries of the Universe and bring them down and share them with humanity, as far as possible, with pure discrimination and with a sense of timing and dosage.

The greater an artist is, the greater a leader is, the deeper is his penetration into higher planes of existence. God-inspired leaders are those who have access into the sphere of the Plan, into the sphere of the Purpose. They know exactly what to do, where, and when. Great ideologies, arts, and sciences are the results of such penetrations.

Within our mental plane we have a twelve-petaled Lotus which, as it unfolds, releases streams of colorful energy into our aura. This Lotus is divided into three parts.[1] Each section has petals with various colors, starting from the center.

A. There are three *knowledge petals*:

- orange — green — violet
- orange — rose — blue
- orange — yellow — indigo

B. There are three *love petals*:

- rose — orange — green — violet
- rose — orange — rose — blue
- rose — orange — yellow — indigo

C. There are three *sacrifice (will) petals*:

- yellow — rose — orange — green — violet
- yellow — orange — violet — rose — blue
- yellow — orange — rose — blue — indigo

The innermost central petals stay closed until a man enters the steps of the Fourth Initiation. Beginning with the Fourth Initiation, these petals unfold, increasing the color of their corresponding petals. When they are fully opened, they radiate an electrical flame of orange-rose and yellow, with such intensity that it burns away the glorious causal body, or Lotus, and releases the hu-

---

1. See also the Chalice section in *The Subconscious Mind and the Chalice.*

man soul to be a *noble,* a Master with a rainbow of many colors around Him.

When the Lotus is destroyed, the Inner Guide departs after giving birth to her baby — the human soul. The human soul is born in fire and through fire; he is a fiery being in the subjective, as well as objective, world. The human soul then enters the Spiritual Triad and radiates triadal colors.

Deep in the Core, he is a Spark. We are red Sparks, blue Sparks, or yellow Sparks, according to our Rays. As the human soul advances toward perfection, the color of the Spark predominates over the colors of the Spiritual Triad. We are told that in the Halls of the Hierarchy and in the Grand Lodge of Shamballa, Initiates are seated according to the intensity and purity of the colors of Their Sparks.

As our auric colors become clearer, purer, and more translucent and radiant, we build closer communication lines with the invisible Hierarchy formed of Its proper colors.

The function of the aura is to

1. absorb and emanate psychic energy
2. register impressions coming from various sources in the Cosmos and corresponding planes
3. act as a communication line with the planes of existence of the Great Ones

4. serve as a vehicle to put the human soul in communication with the corresponding plane of existence
5. protect from psychic and subjective attacks
6. if well organized, repel the attack of germs, microbes, and destructive auras

The aura grows as the human soul expresses greater virtue, organizes his centers on each plane, and changes the focus of his consciousness from a lower to a higher plane. The colors in our aura change, mixing with its natural colors the colors of our virtues and of higher contacts, or mixing our auric colors with the colors of our negative emotions, blind urges and drives, with the colors of our impure thoughts, glamors, illusions, and vanities.

In the etheric level, lust causes a lot of change in color. In the emotional plane there are seven factors which create ugly colors and color formations. These are hatred, fear, anger, jealousy, greed, malice, and slander. On the mental plane, pollution of color begins with thoughts of selfishness, separatism, vanity, hypocrisy, and so on.

Thus, sometimes our aura looks like scintillating colors of great beauty; other times it looks like a sheet of cloth, blotted by grey, brown, or dark spots like a deteriorating rag. These colors not only indicate negative emotions but also criminal thoughts and destructive, selfish motives. Anger is another extremely dangerous force which rends the aura. It looks like lightning, surrounded with red and black colors.

People have many rents in their aura. If the etheric body is torn, astral energy pours in and overstimulates the cells, causing great damage to the body. If the astral body is torn, astral entities can sneak in and obsess or possess your body. If the mental aura is cracked, you are exposed to various kinds of mental disturbances, few of which are curable. If the higher auras are built, they can protect your aura and sometimes patch it.

The corresponding locations of cracks in the body are directly affected.

After being angry, you notice changes in your body, feelings, and thinking. From this you can learn a great lesson.

The condition of the aura directly affects the auras of those who are closest to us. It affects the auras of those with whom we work or relate. Thus, we either bring vitality and joy into the aura of others, or we contaminate them with our aura.

Irritation and depression create cleavages within your entire aura. When cleavages come into being, communion between different parts of the aura is stopped. For example, your emotional aura slowly builds sharp edges; your mental aura develops special border lines. You become a house divided within itself. Such cleavages have a drastic effect on your life. You lose direction; you always change your goals, planes, discussions, and associations and try to manufacture reasons for your conduct.

Depression appears as a great and dark wave in your aura, mixed with murky red. Irritation appears as if your aura is contaminated with scarlet fever, with red and black spots. Fear creates great disturbances in your aura. It appears as a black-grey cloud, or smoggy fog, which spreads all over your aura and paralyzes the pulsations, or breathing, of the aura. Wherever the cloud is thick, the corresponding organ suffers. It generally attacks the heart and kidneys.

Continuity of consciousness is possible only if the components of your overall aura blend and fuse with each other and rhythmically pulsate. Any black spot in your aura stops the circulation of psychic energy. Wherever psychic energy cannot penetrate, decay and disintegration appear.

Negative emotions and thoughts pass from one plane to another. Physical anger appears in the astral and mental planes. Often you cannot enter the higher planes if there is too much agitation in your aura.

After one leaves the physical plane, invisible helpers often take him to the astral plane and give him a strong dose of peace — if the anger he carries is a kind of selfless indignation. There are many invisible helpers who try to clean your aura before you enter the higher spheres, if that pollution in your aura is due to dedicated service and selfless labor among people contaminated with ugly formations of dark colors.

Higher emotions, aspiration, thoughts of compassion and beauty give wings to your aura. For spatial flights, you need wings. As your aura grows and expands, it takes you to faraway places on earth. If it expands further, you experience flights in the solar system.

If our higher bodies are built, we become able to fly to stars and galaxies.

The Spark, throughout ages, is building vehicles to liberate Itself from the captivity of this planet, in order to enjoy Its divine freedom in space. The Spark is born in space; It will return to the freedom of space.

Every color is an octave; therefore, we have twelve octaves. Each color in an octave has a different sound, effect, and form in the aura. Each note in combination with another note either creates harmony or discord.

The eye is more sensitive than the ear, but there are few who can see the scales of the notes and translate them in terms of emotions, thoughts, and motives. Sight is also different on different levels. You can see etherically, astrally, or mentally. All those sights are clouded by the color of the aura through which they watch the auras of others. In even the best cases, their perception is a combination of colors which do not correspond to reality. That is how those who read auras mislead people.

The chemistry of colors in the aura is a very advanced science which has not been written down or given to the public. Every action, emotion, and thought has its own chemistry. The state of our consciousness charges the chemistry of our aura. Just as an expert chemist knows what elements to mix and how to mix them to achieve a certain purpose, an advanced Initiate does the same thing with the chemistry of colors.

In the future, great geniuses will come and they will paint with the knowledge of such esoteric chemistry and bring transformation into the lives of those who will have the great fortune of coming in contact with their works of art.

Advanced music is a dance of colors in space which has a very great therapeutic effect on the aura. Those auras which are blocked with glamors, illusions, crystallizations of desires, posthypnotic suggestions, fear, anger, crime, jealousy, greed, and so on violently reject pure music and choose those kinds of music which excite or protect these ugly formations. Pure, esoterically-prepared, higher music or paintings can cure such individuals, if they endure the painful process of the harmonization of their aura through purification. Esoterically-prepared music chooses those notes (colors) which will vitalize the higher bodies, devitalize closed formations, and bring the true keynote of the person forward by playing the keynote of his birth, or his rising sign if he is above-average.

The chemistry of colors for each person is different, and each month it is different for every person.

Zodiacal signs hit the chords. Every month there is a different chord, and the esoteric musician who is working to heal a person will use the keynote of the month, in harmony with the keynote of the person's birth or rising sign.

Many different colored waves appear in the aura for a few seconds or days, and then disappear. These colorful waves are produced by our thoughts, emotions, urges and drives. According to their intensity, they create their own colors. Sometimes the colors are very complex, due to the complexity of feelings and thoughts.

Some of these impermanent waves of color pollute certain parts of the aura for a long time. Some of them bring new vitality to the entire aura. We call these latter the benevolent waves or the nourishers. It is the nourishers which bring vitality and healing to the entire mechanism.

Our aura often reflects the conditions of the aura of those who are close to us. Sometimes the auras of our closest ones either infect or invigorate our aura. Infection of the aura is a fact. The aura is sometimes infected long before physical infection has occurred. Protective measures in the aura are those waves of color which emanate from our love, gratitude, solemnity, lofty thoughts, honesty, nobility, and enthusiasm. Such waves are disinfecting and invigorating.

Some people have rhythmically palpitating waves in their aura, which are protectors. These protectors, like white blood cells, are attracted to polluted locations in the aura and clear them away. Protectors are the forces generated from ideas and thoughts related to Infinity, holism, and the One Self.

There are other kinds of waves in the aura which act as repulsers. Repulsers can be good or bad. Sometimes they repulse moral and spiritual intruders; sometimes they repulse the beneficent currents of higher wisdom or the waves of new direction.

Good repulsers are generated by the standards we have in our higher mind or in moments of intuitive contemplation. Bad repulsers are those which are produced by our prejudices and superstitions; these automatically reject any waves that do not synchronize with their color or vibration. Bad repulsers can be defeated through right education and through expansion of consciousness.

Thus, the aura is a very active field of electromagnetic, colorful waves. The most beautiful auras are those which in some way attract rays from space. Sometimes the aura serves as a prism to these rays and glows with new colors. These rays come from great initiates, from angels, devas, and from Those Who live in Their Nirvanic or higher bodies. We call these rays *spatial rivers of beauty*.

These rays are attracted by those who are pure in heart. The electrical sphere of a pure heart radiates the most gorgeous color formations in the aura, like a diamond shining the light of the heart. In certain moments of life, it spreads like a shield all over the human aura. The light of the heart carries a great voltage of healing energy.

Sometimes a person is healed instantaneously from so-called incurable diseases by the light of the heart. The light of the heart is the transmitter of psychic energy, which not only burns away any kind of pollution but also harmonizes and regulates the centers and orchestrates all the colors into a symphony.

The human soul, being a white light, can color the aura through any color by using thought energy. Once the human soul redeems himself from the chains of illusion, glamor, and maya, he is a great alchemist of colors.

Through various combinations of color, he can bring healing to the personality vehicles and expand the consciousness, making the human aura vibrate in the resonance of higher spheres.

One of the colors that the human soul uses is violet. In creating a violet color within the aura, the human soul brings harmony and healing in the aura by attracting certain healing devas, the violet devas. The color violet is closely related to the etheric body. Defects in the etheric body can be healed by the color violet, or by sounding the note which corresponds to the color violet.

The human soul can also put the aura in contact with green devas, who work on the mental plane, spreading the color green into the aura. A green aura can be used to transmit precious knowledge from higher planes.

Deformity in our physical body comes into being when our mother's aura was deformed during pregnancy by various causes, or if the records of the three permanent atoms contain deformed images or seeds from previous lives. When a person is ready to incarnate, the light of the human soul hits the permanent atoms and creates exactly corresponding images on the screen of the physical existence, like a negative. The permanent atoms project that which is recorded in them from past thoughts, feelings, and actions. Our permanent atoms contain the blueprint of our future bodies. Defects or deformities in our bodies are the result of violations of the laws of Nature, especially the Law of Love.

People think that only the physical body can be deformed. We will be surprised when we reach the Subtle

Worlds and see deformed astral and mental bodies around us. Evil people have very deformed subtle bodies. This is why you are deeply afraid of them when you see them in your dreams.

The damage that we do to others, we also do to ourselves. For example, if I stab you with a knife, in that instance I identify with you and your pain. When this happens, the knife is also in my body, in the records. The wound I create in you will be projected in my body the next time I take incarnation. People create deformity in their own nature by trying to deform the mental, emotional, or physical bodies of others. Other agents of deformity are malice, slander, and gossip.

Every time we incarnate, we go to the window of karma to take a look at our account. If we are not too full of debt, karmic law activates our permanent records, and we take an incarnation that pays in the right degree for the violations of any law we have committed.

Sometimes people are born defective because their mothers used drugs or lived in other unwholesome ways. When this happens, people think that the real cause of the deformity is the mother. This may be partly true, but if the incarnating soul had no "tax" problems with the mother or with the law, he would not incarnate through her.

A person "takes a picture" in his mind of whatever he does consciously. This picture, or impression, is already in his permanent atoms. He may forget about the picture, but it is recorded. If it is a destructive picture, it will create a destructive image, or vehicle, in the next incarnation, or it will be a disturbing factor in his consciousness. To have a good future, we must sow seeds in our consciousness or in our permanent atoms. This is so simple.

Some people think that holy or advanced people must have had bad karma because of the suffering through which they often pass. This is not totally true. For example, it may be that they had debts in the past which they did not pay, but now because they are "wealthy," they are able to pay those debts.

It is also true that Holy Ones often suffer not because of their own karma but because of the karma of those related to them in some way. Such Holy Ones consciously suffer for us to pay our karma and enable us to find the path of righteousness, or to pay our debts by helping and serving others.

Some Holy Ones suffer because they overload their circuits. They burn their centers and vehicles by using them excessively in service. Many Holy Ones burn their throat centers and other centers in spreading so much psychic energy, depriving themselves by helping others. They do this out of compassion, knowing that the troubles of this life are nothing compared to the blessings they will share in the Subtle Worlds.

No advanced disciple exists unless he has cleaned his past karma. It is therefore most probable that the Great Ones suffer because of the above-mentioned reasons. Every great service one renders is because of the absence of bad karma.

It is possible to have high-level certificates and knowledge, but if your karma is heavy, you are prevented from entering the field of true service. Discipline, study, and education cannot make you a server, unless you have paid your past karma. If your karma has not been worked out, and if you force yourself into a high position, you become a very destructive and dangerous agent to the masses.

Your karma must be clear before you are led into the field of true service. Every sacrificial service we render to humanity expands in the future into a greater field of service for us.

We can eliminate our karma by the following methods:

- living a life of beauty, goodness, righteousness, joy, and freedom
- walking in the steps of Christ, as all Great Ones do
- increasing our sacrificial service to humanity
- exercising right thinking, right feeling, right speech, and right action
- loving others more than ourselves
- developing virtues and eliminating vices, habits, and hang-ups
- developing discrimination in the hearts of our children, inspiring them toward right, and challenging them to transcend their limitations

If all of our parents had been good examples for us, and if we had been good examples for our children, humanity would now be a part of the "Kingdom of God." If we had taught our children the Law of Karma and made them understand that whatever they sow, they reap, we would not be living in such dangerous conditions on earth.

Nothing that is developed artificially will exist after death, except the damage that has been done by it. All artificial methods must be eliminated, and one must engage himself in purifying and expanding his consciousness by living a life of Beauty, Goodness, Righteousness, Joy, Freedom, Striving, and Sacrificial Service.

Chapter 4

The Etheric Body

The etheric body has four dimensions or extensions. The lowest one is between the physical body and the astral body. It prevents astral forces from burning the physical body and prematurely flowing into it. The next one separates the astral body from the mental body, with the same purpose. The next one divides the lower and higher minds. Then there is one between the mental body and the Intuitional body.

These etheric layers are protective networks, like bumpers or shock-absorbers. Any violent movement on any level is restricted to that level, in order not to hurt the lower level or the higher level. Thus, a violent emotional reaction does not immediately destroy the mind or the physical body because of the etheric layers. However, if it is repeated, it hurts the related bodies.

Sometimes when we are in the astral plane, we pass through violent storms or fights. But such an agitation or tension does not hurt the physical body or the mental body because of etheric insulation. But if a person is an Initiate, these etheric webs are eliminated or are very thin, and any violent action in any body affects the other bodies very strongly.

In a way, the physical body of an Initiate is vulnerable through his subtle bodies, although sometimes he is protected by the shield of the One under Whose command he works and fights against the forces of darkness.

If someone shoots you in the Subtle World with astral weapons, you will develop a wound in the corresponding place in your physical body. If there is a crack between the astral and physical planes, you are physically in danger. If there is a crack between the astral and mental planes, you are emotionally unbalanced and crazy. If a crack exists between the lower and higher minds, you are in total confusion between what is abstract and what is concrete; you are a mentally-suspended being who is neither in contact with heaven nor the world. Thousands of such people are found in various yoga groups, churches, and so-called New-Age groups.

When there is a crack between the Intuitional Plane and the mental plane, you are the best customer for psychiatrists and a ripe candidate for an asylum. Hallucination results from such a crack.

Curiously enough, our advancement depends upon creating a passage between the planes so that our consciousness can travel in any plane without creating problems. Such a passage is called the Antahkarana, the Golden Bridge, or continuity of consciousness. This passage has controlling valves, which one closes after he passes into a higher level. Unless such a passage or communication line between the physical brain and higher planes is established, one can never advance on the path of perfection and bring the treasures of higher realms to this world.

Chapter 5

The Sacred Word and the Aura

We must use the sacred word for purification, release, recharging, and actualization. The first step is to sit relaxed and focused in your highest consciousness. Then, remember the note of your sun sign or rising sign (see page 15).

If you are trying to

   a. purify your aura
   b. release yourself, the human soul, from glamor, illusion, and maya
   c. fuse with the revealing, expanding forces of Nature

then, using the note of the rising sign and visualizing its color, sound each syllable of the sacred word OM for ten seconds, thus:

- O — ten seconds
- M — ten seconds

If you are trying to:

a. actualize an idea
b. bring construction and organization into being
c. recharge your etheric body and aura

then, using your sun-sign note and its color, take a deep breath and in a very relaxed way sound each syllable of the sacred word, AUM, for ten seconds, thus:

- A — ten seconds
- U — ten seconds
- M — ten seconds

Each time the sacred word must be sounded three, five, or seven times. Start with three times. Then five months later increase to five times. Then seven months later increase to seven times.

It will be a great advantage for you if you meditate for five minutes on the virtue of your rising or sun sign, according to the sacred word you are using that day.

After a few years of experience, you can use the *chord* for your rising or sun sign, with three colors of the chord.

For the rising sign, sound three OMs, using the first note of the chord for the first OM, the second note for the second OM, and the third note for the third OM, visualizing the proper color for each note, and focusing mentally on the corresponding virtue.

For the sun sign, sound the first syllable of AUM using the first note and color, the second syllable using the second note and color, and the third syllable using the third note and color, taking one breath for each syllable, as follows:

- A — one breath, ten seconds
- U — one breath, ten seconds
- M — one breath, ten seconds

Then take one breath for the sacred word as a whole. Repeat AUM three times using this method. Use the same breathing method for OM.[1]

The aura can be stabilized through various means. Will power can stabilize the etheric and physical aura. Thoughts can stabilize the emotional aura. The mental aura can be stabilized with intuitional light. Irritation or nervousness makes your aura agitated. Once your aura is agitated, you are subject to any "push-buttons" in your nature. Push-buttons are crystallized patterns in your aura which gain power every time you are irritated, angry, or nervous. They make you lose control of your aura.

For example, if you are afraid to give a lecture, fear makes you nervous. Because you want to talk but you have fear, nervousness agitates your aura and you par-

---

1. WARNING: Use of the sacred word in this way may bring great changes within you and within your environment. Do this exercise only once a day.

tially lose control of what you intended to say. In such cases it is better to stop the fear through the use of logic or visualization exercises.

Whenever the aura is calm, it allows you to speak the way you want. Your aura literally expresses and conveys your visions, dreams, and spiritual joy to the auras of others before they sense it in your voice. Whenever you are imparting lofty ideas related to beauty, goodness, truth, Infinity, you expand your aura and feed the aura of the audience.

There are many kinds of auras. Some of them sap you; some of them feed your deepest aspirations. Your aura can always be charged when you think or speak about beauty, goodness, truth, joy, and gratitude. Gratitude especially is a great vitamin for your aura.

The aura of a human being may be cleaned of crystallized formations through music. I have written certain music which, if listened to carefully for a period of five months, will dissolve many kinds of glamors, illusions, and maya. The process of cleansing is as follows.

First, the music will create a repulsive reaction, if the layers of crystallization are thick. Then dislocation occurs and the crystallizations move to the surface of the aura. At this point they lose their sharp borders and become cloud-like masses. It is at this point that the music begins to create a slight sensation of joy. After feeling such joy, the process of dissolving the crystallizations increases and continues.

During the period of breaking the crystallizations, a person passes through crises. Eventually, emotional and mental stabilization takes place with an increasing amount of health and energy.

When the crystallizations are finally melted, intense love for the music appears in the heart of the person. This takes a few months, but eventually the aura shines with its normal colors.

The way to listen to this music is to relax and let the sound of the music penetrate your entire aura, until you almost memorize the music and mentally follow it. The pieces of music to which I refer are[2]

1. Waiting for Dawn
2. Sirius
3. Sedona
4. Stars
5. At the Gate of Shamballa (or Vision)
6. Far-Off Mountains
7. Spring of Colors
8. Flying Cranes and Blooming Orchids
9. Dance of Swallows
10. Fire Dragon
11. Leo Sunrise
12. Blue Aquarius

This must be listened to for twenty minutes every evening before sleeping, and on Sundays when you have

---

2. These pieces can be found in the music CD and cassettes composed and performed by the author.

time for retreat or seclusion. It is more effective during the night or during the day in Nature.

As a magnet rearranges iron filings in the pattern of the magnetic rays, so music arranges the atoms of the aura. As these atoms arrange and rearrange, they free themselves from the power of crystallization, and eventually all the auric waves flow in harmonious rhythm with each other. Physical, emotional, and mental health depend on how synchronously and harmoniously the atoms and cells circulate in the aura.

Music not only heals; it is also a source of many mental and moral disorders. The world's economy is even influenced by music. There is music which leads the economy toward depression, and there is music which leads to prosperity. This may sound insane to those who have never raised their eyes from the earth, but those who are open and intuitively free can grasp the implications.

We must remember that our aura is a cell in the aura of the planet. The planetary aura is an aggregate of the auras of all forms living on the planet. Your aura is not only related to your body but also to your family, wife, husband, and to humanity. That is why it is a basic truth that man is one with humanity. There is the solar aura and the galactic aura. Man is related to all; all is related to man. This is the foundation of the thought that there is one Unity.

Just as our aura has its own note, the planetary aura has its own note and color. The Solar Lord is playing His music on twelve planetary notes. The goal of each person is to make that solar music echo in his own tiny aura and find creative expression through it, until "as above, so below" is realized and actualized.

Babies must be born in auras that form a symphony to attract an advanced soul. At the time of making love, your aura is visible to those whose time has come for incarnation. Advanced souls choose those auras which are colorful, pure, and symphonic. Retarded souls feel rejection from highly developed auras; they choose the chaotic auras created by rape, at the time of unwilling sex, or sex which is carried out in irritation, worry, in criminal moods, or on lower levels of evolution.

Knowing these facts, the ancients stressed that marriage is sacred and that it must be sanctified by meditation, prayers, and the blessings of those who live in high spiritual principles. Ceremonies, prayers, blessings, love, and understanding help the auras mix and blend and become highly magnetic for advanced souls.

The fusion of the auras depends on the level of the couple. If only their physical auras mix during love-making, they will attract low-level souls. If their mental, intuitional, or higher auras blend, they will attract higher and more advanced souls. Talents and geniuses are born during a moment of highest fusion of auras.

If the crime in a nation is increasing, it means that people are mating on lower levels, only for fun, and are bringing in low and unevolved, premature souls. People seek the causes of crime elsewhere, but the greatest crime is to bring in an immature soul and raise him in an environment that will not give him an opportunity to grow and will influence him to exercise immorality over others.

Our auras can be polluted, just as the aura of our planet is polluted. Any pollution of the planetary aura has disastrous consequences on the forms living on the planet. The rays of the Sun bring not only life but also wisdom and direction. When the aura of the planet is filled with layers of pollution hundreds of miles thick, these rays cannot reach us in their purity. Instead, they come to us in a chemistry that creates various sicknesses and insanity of many kinds.

Unfortunately, the aura of our planet is already in very bad shape. Only those who have higher antennas, higher bodies, are able to keep their direction toward the Solar Purpose, though their bodies suffer. This condition will continue until a great catastrophe once again cleans the earth and its aura. Such a catastrophe is not just a possibility but an inevitable fate, waiting for the right moment to prove the stupidity of greed, materialism, and separatism.

Such crises appear in the human aura, in smaller cycles. We call these "cycles of misfortune, sickness, disease, and death." These cycles bring a new opportunity for a person to live more intelligently and in greater harmony with the Divine Intent.

Just as in the days of Lot, it will really be five or ten righteous people who will be able to sustain the life of this planet, bringing new life through their far-reaching spiritual rays. But when these righteous souls depart, we will witness a new Sodom and Gomorrah on Earth.

Purification of the human aura is possible to a certain degree. The physical and etheric aura can be purified by eating clean food, breathing pure air, and drinking clean water. The emotional aura can be purified by increasing love and compassion, and expressing them in all relationships. The fire of love is a purifying factor. The mental aura can be purified when one does not yield to lies, hypocrisy, deceit, flattery, vanity, prejudice, or pride.

All these methods mean that purification takes place from within. The higher mind can exercise a great influence on the purification process, if you hold the ideas and visions of synthesis and unity in it.

Thoughts, emotions, words, and deeds can purify or pollute your aura. They are the effects of emanating rays of energy. The source of that energy, the controlling center, must radiate pure, positive, and constructive energy to purify the aura.

The Core of the human being contains many virtues. As these virtues manifest, they not only purify the whole person, but they also make his aura a magnetic mirror which reflects all that is going on in higher planes. All Great Ones emphasized the virtues as the most concrete foundation of life. When virtues increase, the pollution of our aura will vanish, and the pollution of the planet will come under our control.

Colors and notes, if used esoterically and with intelligent arrangement, create that atmosphere or those conditions in which the manifestation of virtue becomes easier. Electrification, or recharging, of the aura is possible through the following means:

1. Continuous labor and striving for the betterment of life
2. Devotion to higher ideals
3. Meditation on the laws and principles of the New Era
4. Sacrificial service in daily life
5. Development of will through endurance, patience, and steady perseverance to radiate your inner beauty through virtues
6. Living, thinking, and talking always in purity
7. Trying to raise your consciousness as high as possible to register the wisdom of Great Ones

True nobility is not in our positions, ranks, or casts. True nobility is manifestation of our innermost Self, which naturally creates around our body the Robe of Glory. Living and moving in such a rainbow robe is nobility.

Chapter 6

Changes of Color in the Aura

The aura demonstrates an ever-changing state of colors. Some of these changes are improvements; others are signs of degeneration. Some of the colors fight and create discord. Some of them show harmony.

The basic colors of the heart and Chalice act as principles or keynotes against which we have the colors emanating from various centers and bodies. Their colors are the way they express their inner urges and drives, desires, aspirations, and striving.

Each color is a manifestation of a motive, mood, state of consciousness, bliss, ecstasy, or a higher or lower contact. It may even be a manifestation of impressions coming from various sources. All these impressions cause changes in the existing colors of the aura, or add new colors or shades to it.

Stability is a very important word in the science of the aura. Stability is the condition of the aura in which a few powerful colors dominate, forming a chord of colors as if they were notes. When these colors reach a state which cannot be disturbed by other fluctuations, we say that the aura has reached a state of stability. Stability is also a powerful field of radioactive energy that repulses certain impressions coming from outside which are not in harmony with the predominating colors.

Impressions, influences, and contacts bring health or sickness into the aura, according to the vibrations they carry. Every force and every kind of energy in the form of emotion, thought, or motive affect the aura, for good or for bad.

An evil thought can turn into a destructive factor in the aura of another person and eventually lead him into certain diseases. Similarly, a blessing or bliss can penetrate into the aura and destroy harmful waves existing in it.

The contents of the aura condition the failure or success of the person. "Good seeds" blossom into flowers; "bad seeds" become destructive factors in the life of the person.

Stabilization is a state of continuous flow and harmony. Stabilization is attained when the human soul takes the Third Initiation, in which he radiates his glory in the aura. Another stage of stabilization is reached when a person's consciousness functions in the Spiritual Triad. The higher the beingness of a person climbs, the more stability is seen in the aura.

Eventually the aura becomes a wheel of twelve spokes which revolve at such an incredible speed that it appears as if the wheel is standing still, and all twelve rays are clearly seen. This stage is the stage of glory, or we say that the person now wears the Robe of Glory.

The health aura is not the radiation of any vehicle or center but is a manifestation of pranic energy on the surface of the body. The etheric spleen receives the prana, distributes it throughout the etheric network into the human body, and manifests it as a particular radiation on the surface of the body, which is called the health aura. It is called the health aura because the health of the body depends on the proper intake of prana and the proper circulation of prana in the body.[1]

When the health aura appears stable and radiant, we say that the person is healthy. Such a health aura is the result of many factors, such as

1. proper circulation of prana in the etheric and physical bodies
2. harmony between the etheric body and the astral and mental bodies
3. the presence of certain devas who contribute to forming the health aura

This aura appears thickened on the surface of the body as the etheric body withdraws itself from the physical body during the time of death. The health aura is also

---

1. See *New Dimensions in Healing* chapters on etheric body and prana, and refer to Ch. 115, "Glory in Man," in *The Psyche and Psychism*.

a shield against germs and microbes in the aura. Being electrical in nature, the health aura can burn many microbes and germs flying in the atmosphere.

What is the color of the aura when you pass away? First, if your subtle bodies, such as your astral and mental bodies, are organized, you will have an astral and mental aura; but if they are not yet all built or mature, you will have mixed colors. If your mental body is built, in the astral plane your mental color predominates.

There is a state in the Subtle Worlds called "nudity" or "nakedness" which happens when you have ruined your subtle bodies or sold them to evil. In the Subtle Worlds, the color of your aura and its measure are what express the degree of your advancement on the Path. People see you exactly as you are, even your moral wounds and ulcers in your subtle bodies.[2]

People think that they are already in higher spheres when they sleep. But the truth is that this earthbound humanity is usually nowhere else but in its pajamas. One must have developed subtle bodies in order to travel, and subtle bodies are built throughout many incarnations dedicated to aspiration and striving.

Some people want to see the aura. Part of it can be detected by electronic instruments, but if one develops higher clairvoyance, he will see the aura as clearly as he sees physical objects with his physical eyes. Clairvoyance cannot be developed artificially or by working on

---

2. See also *Other Worlds*, especially chapters on the Mental and Astral Planes.

the centers but by living a life of renunciation and service. Clairvoyance is like a flower which at first was a seed buried in the earth but which, in time, surfaces and blooms — if conditions are favorable. All true psychic gifts are naturally-bloomed flowers, the result of lives lived in striving and sacrificial service.

How We Harm the Aura

There are things that are harmful to the aura. For example, drugs, tobacco, marijuana, and alcohol are physical things which are very harmful to the aura; these weaken or destroy parts of the aura. Excessive sex also saps the aura. Sleeplessness is very dangerous to the aura.

Jealousy, the spirit of revenge, fear, hatred, and fanaticism are emotional conditions which harm the aura. They poison it and weaken the immune system of the body. Malice, slander, and treason act as disintegrative poisons in the aura, preparing it for obsession and possession, especially when they are amplified through spoken words.

Evil, destructive, and selfish thoughts, thoughts based on separatism, lies, and fabrications, and thoughts that are manipulative can ruin the mental aura and make the body susceptible to various infections.

People think that they are spiritually advanced because they read various religious books or help people in certain ways. But in reality, people advance only if they daily renew their auras through lofty thinking, loving emotions, and the rendering of harmless, sacrificial service. One may talk nicely, but if he has hidden motives he becomes insincere — a hypocrite. Sincerity is the ability to manifest your inner, lofty motives or intentions, exactly as they are.

People think that talking openly about their bad intentions, feelings, or actions is an act of sincerity. But sincerity is a virtue. How can you be a thief and in the meantime be an honest person? Sincerity is related to the expression of your inner beauty, not to hiding your responses or reactions to other people's thoughts, feelings, and actions. A sincere person is one who shines his light without hindering it or hiding it.

Jealousy is a craving for those things that people have, feeling that others should not have what they do. Sometimes jealousy leads to destructive action to take what others have, or to destroy the object of desire or the owner of the object of desire. This creates a very disturbing condition in the aura, that eventually produces various psychological and physical ailments.

No one can advance on the path of perfection if he carries jealousy in his heart. One must watch how jealousy sneaks into his words, feelings, actions, and thoughts through various means and pretensions. Jealousy is a disintegrating factor in the aura.

The spirit of revenge, fear, hatred, and fanaticism create a similar effect in the aura. They are like termites in the aura. Hatred creates a toxin in the aura which eats a part of the aura and stops the free flow of pranic energy in the aura and to the corresponding parts of the physical body.

The whole aura is an interwoven network of threads through which life-energy circulates. Breaking this network produces severe health problems. If the aura is healthy and harmonious, the health aura appears and, like a shield, protects the physical body from any arrows that are directed toward it. Arrows are the negative and harmful thoughts, emotions, and emanations that are all around us.

Anger breaks the sphere of the aura and opens cracks used for the invasion of dark forces. After the aura is cracked, one no longer has any immunity to germs or various entities which try to take over the body.

The Great Ones advise us to keep people who are polluted with jealousy, hatred, and anger away from sacred places and sacred service. These elements not only pollute the sphere where higher service is rendered, but the people also hurt themselves, exposing themselves to the reaction of the Forces of Light which function in these spheres.

Fear paralyzes the petals of the chakras, making them look like leaves burned by the scorching sun. When the petals are paralyzed, a person is in the process of dying. Fear kills people; leaders who lead people through various fear techniques soon find themselves surrounded by sick, insane people.

Revenge brings to the aura all those elements that were once expelled from the aura. The physical body is not the only mechanism that eliminates by-products or waste elements that are no longer needed by the body;

the etheric, astral, and mental mechanisms also eliminate whatever is dead or harmful to retain. Revenge returns these elements to the aura, and very soon you notice that a degenerative process is going on in your physical, emotional, and mental bodies.

The danger is that when the higher bodies are degenerated, you take them with you into the Higher Worlds and live a miserable life there, then incarnate later with damaged bodies. Every action of revenge pumps previously eliminated elements back into the aura. Groups and nations destroy their auras and prepare a very dark future for themselves if they act with the evil of revenge. If we study the history of humanity in a pure light, this can be seen very clearly.

Remorse is defined as self-reproach which is excited by a sense of guilt. The opposite of remorse is a clear and pure self-examination that is not related to guilt but to the causes which created remorse and with the intent to remove those causes. Remorse creates conflicting, contradictory waves in the aura, which create chaos within the person's thinking, feeling, and actions. The higher Self tries to send regenerating thoughts, but these thoughts meet and are repelled by the waves of guilt feelings.

The ego creates a big tumor in your aura that devours most of your energy, swells up, and eventually stands against the human soul, the real you. When the ego is big enough, you become your own enemy, always changing your viewpoints and decisions from your Real Self to the ego, and then from the ego to the Real Self.

The ego creates a pendulum in you which fluctuates between two points. Eventually your ego grows so big that the Real Self almost vanishes. Because an ego is a programmed center, your life falls into the hands of a machine.

Vanity is also very damaging to the aura. Vanity disfigures the aura, which is normally an egg-shaped sphere, and makes it irregular in shape with heavy condensations in certain places. When vanity increases, the aura is pulled up toward the head, way above the head, leaving only a very faint mist of aura around the lower part of the body. Because of this dislocation of the aura, various chakras in the three bodies cannot influence their exact counterparts in the physical body, and inner chaos results. The sense of reality disappears, and a person lives in his "imaginary castles." Such a person is not only unhealthy but a danger to society as well.

Vanity and ego require Herculean efforts to destroy. But if you have a real Teacher who does not manipulate your weaknesses, he can help you get rid of them, if you are sincere in your decision to go forward on the spiritual path. The Teacher's technique will be a direct confrontation with you and your ego to make you see that you are not your ego but the human soul. He will destroy the artificially built images and vanities and free you to be your Self. But very few people choose to go through the suffering to lose their ego and vanity.

When your evolution stops because of your ego and vanity, life either sends you a Teacher or humiliates you to break them. Sometimes the Teacher appears in forms you do not expect. He can be a cruel boss who always puts his finger on your wounds and tries to make you see what you really are. He can be your husband or wife, or a friend who drives you crazy because of your ego and vanity. Sometimes he can be your child. If you realize the opportunity and drop your ego and vanity, you will see a great change in your consciousness. Your aura will become harmonious, peaceful, and beautiful, and your Teacher will change into a loving person.

Self-interest has a very peculiar effect on the aura. It creates many whirlpools in your aura, each one of which represents a focus of interest. Whenever you relate to other people, these whirlpools suck their auras into your aura. People around you feel sapped, and you collect not only their energy but also the glamors and weaknesses in their auras.

Self-interested people gradually lose right judgment and develop confused minds that seek to manipulate people in order to add to their own interest. Eventually the aura can no longer nourish the whirlpools, and they turn into wounds. Anything that runs against such a person's self-interest causes pain in them. These pains gradually manifest in the bones and in the body in the form of various diseases.

The next element is servility. Servility is submissiveness, a "yes, sir" attitude, a slavish attitude. The person does anything for you that you expect, but with a hidden motive to knock you down at the right time. A servile person manipulates you with his "yes, sir" attitude. Most people open their doors to servile people because such people nourish their egos. Most people enjoy having a slave, but the slave slowly gains their confidence and penetrates into all their secrets. Once power is given to them, they turn into embodiments of revenge toward their masters.

Servility brings certain motions into the etheric body which are harmonious with the etheric aura of the master, but then it creates motions and colors in the emotional and/or mental aura that are opposite to and inharmonious with the motions of the etheric body of the master. This factor sometimes manifests as doubt in the heart of the master toward the servile person, but, because the actions of the servile person are more visible than the effects created by his emotional and mental aura, the master continues to enjoy the servility of the person.

Such a relationship hurts both people. The servile person suddenly develops deep inertia not only physically but emotionally and mentally as well. Two contradictory motions create retardation in the flow of his aura, and eventually he does not want to think, feel, or act.

Servility can be destroyed by trying to be sincere and noble. Our aura is nourished when our thoughts, feelings, and actions come from our inner Core, which is pure bliss, joy, compassion, and light.

The predominating color of the aura is the color of the vehicle in which the consciousness is focused. Consciousness activates that body and makes it radiate powerful streams of color into the aura. When the consciousness shifts from one level to another, or from one plane to another, it creates corresponding changes of color in the aura.

There are eight languages through which a human being communicates:

1. movement, motion
2. smell
3. voice, sound
4. words
5. colors
6. symbols, geometric forms
7. telepathy
8. impression

Higher souls read us continuously because they know all languages. The higher one goes, the more languages he uses, according to those with whom he communicates. When the aura achieves stability, it receives all impressions like a mirror and translates them in a way that we are ready to understand. Understanding is the result of the correct translation of impressions.

Our etheric and astral bodies are egg-shaped around the body. The mental body appears as a sphere of light, starting above the head and reaching a little below the heart. The Intuitional body appears like a midnight-blue halo. The Atmic body appears as rays of diamonds. The Monadic body appears as an indigo star. The Divine body appears like a ruby flame. All of their radiations flow into the aura and condition its coloring.

Many things can change the color of the aura, for bad or for good. For example, handshakes and kisses change the aura. A violent change takes place during intercourse. Looks can change the aura. As we look at someone, streams of subtle energy pour out of our eyes. The eyes channel etheric, astral, and mental energy and sometimes the force of glamor, illusion, ego, or vanity, causing changes in the auras of others.

Love can flow out of your aura, as well as streams of lust, hatred, and fear. In olden days, young girls were advised not to look into the eyes of men in order not to be caught in the influence of their sexual urges or other emotions. In some places on earth, women still veil their eyes as a protection against the energy of lust pouring out from men in general.

The eyes not only pour out energy, but they also magnetically receive energy. The eyes can also radiate healing energy, wisdom, courage, and pure love, although to radiate such energies one must be victorious over his lower nature. Your eyes radiate the color changes in your aura. This is why the eye is called the mirror of the total man.

The aura is affected by the fragrance of flowers, trees, and vegetation, as well as by pollution, chemicals, precious stones, bad smells, noise, or explosions. Explosions have a very destructive effect upon the aura. The sounds made by guns, bombs, and other explosives and collisions are a direct cause of the commission of crime and insanity in the world.

The company of certain people can affect your aura. If you are in the presence of an advanced human being, your aura improves. When you are in the presence of a criminal or an earthbound man, your aura weakens and loses its beauty. This is why we are told to be always in good company and choose our friends from people who are striving toward perfection.

Deep breathing of the pure air found in mountains and deserts changes the aura. Actually, breathing has a great influence upon the aura. Shallow breathing, long breathing, shaky breathing, fearful breathing, lusty breathing, and so on, all affect the aura differently. One must learn to breathe deeply. However, even deep breathing cannot sublimate the aura if one does not also concentrate his mind on a vision or great idea or feel beauty, joy, and freedom. Only by focusing one's mind on great ideas during breathing does one cause positive changes in the aura.

We are not referring to breathing exercises, which can be very dangerous. We are referring to normal deep breathing.

Choosing Colors to Wear

You can choose the color of your clothing by the predominating color in your aura. But how can you know what color this is? If you have no higher clairvoyance, you must see which colors really attract you, especially in flowers and sunsets, and then try that color. If any color irritates you or creates negative emotions or harmful words, change that color. But you must observe the color for a long time in order to make a good choice. This is because there is a danger of error in your choice.

You often have changing moods. Each mood is a color. If you choose a color while you are in changing moods, you make a wrong choice. This is why you sometimes buy a piece of clothing, and then hate it two days later.

The colors that create the least resistance are black and white. This is why most religious orders choose either black or white. Some sacred brotherhoods use yellow. Yellow can be the dominating color of the head center. If the head centers of the members are active, wearing yellow increases their influence immensely. But if a person who does not have an active head center joins that brotherhood, he harms himself by dressing in yellow because yellow prematurely stimulates his head center and creates imbalance in his system — unless the dominating color in his aura is yellow. One may have yellow predominating in his aura if his soul is Third Ray.

We cannot activate any center by changing the outer colors we wear, but we may create either harmony or reactions in other centers. All true changes come from the unfolding centers and from an expanding consciousness.

Transmutation in the aura resembles a pool of water which slowly becomes pure because new streams of clean water pour in and wash away any old, murky water until the whole pool is turned into a mirror of water. This imagery helps us understand the process, but, in reality, transmutation is a process of release from the limitations of the lower levels and an entering into the freedom of higher spheres.

Transmutation eventually leads to that phenomenon, or state of beingness, which we call Transfiguration, in which the whole aura and the human form become radioactive.

After centuries, Transfiguration culminates in Resurrection. In this event the nucleus is released from the aura, from all the vehicles of the person, and turns into a sphere of glorious light beyond the limitations of time and space — as we understand these terms within the sphere of the Cosmic Physical Plane, or within the sphere of our brain.

There are five supreme signs which show the progress of the evolving aura. When a man is advancing, a blue light comes into being in the aura above the head. This light gradually turns into a five-pointed star, and later into a seven-pointed star. Sometimes, instead of the star, the spark develops into a shaft of light, sometimes referred to as "the sword of warriors." The sword or star shines predominantly with indigo colors and with shades of violet, yellow, and white.

There is also the phenomenon of a blue ring around the head when the Intuitional body comes into formation, and fusion with the higher levels of the mental body takes place. It is this ring that transmits the light of Intuition and enlightens the path of the disciple.

In ancient writings we can find passages describing how the glory of the Lord shone, or of the glory of angels that appeared, the glory of heavenly hosts. The glory to which they refer was a special kind of highly developed aura formed by many colors and radiations.

The glorification of the aura begins with purification of the aura, in which the colors achieve their maximum translucency and stability. Then, the blue ring appears around the head, as depicted in ancient paintings. This ring expands and is filled with a pure orange color in the form of a disk which extends from the head to the lower back behind the spine. This is called "the shield" in some esoteric literature. It protects the person from any kind of psychic attack. This shield looks like plumage with splendid colors. When it reaches its pure tonality, it releases the fires of the etheric, astral, and mental centers and the Chalice, which radiates as twelve ray-colors from the heart, around the entire aura. This is what glory is.

Glory is a condition in which the intuitional blue ring, the atmic orange shield, and the twelve radiations of the Chalice, are united in the fire of the pure Self.

In the Ageless Wisdom we are told that whenever such a glory appeared, people immediately fell prostrate and kept their eyes down, as they could not look at the glory of the colors and the immense beauty expressed. Glory is the color, the radiation, the dynamism, and the overwhelming beauty of the aura.

Significance of Various Colors

Color	*Significance*
Shades of red	Lust
	Will
	Anger
	Spiritual direction
	Purpose
	Vitality
	Vivification
Bright brick red	Anger
Carmine	Pure affection
Red, mixed with smoke	Affection mixed with sensuality
	Lust
Scarlet	Pride
	Solemnity
	Royalty
Deep red, mottled with medium brown	Sensuality
Rose	Unselfish affection
	Compassion
Rose, mixed with red-brown	Selfish affection
Pure orange	Highest intellect
	Sanity
	Health

Red-orange	Intellect Pride Ambition

Orange, mixed with
  brick red
	Low type of
	  intellect

Shades of yellow	Intellectualism Concentration Control of mind and thought
Golden yellow	Wisdom
Pure yellow	Pure intelligence
Shades of blue	Religious aspiration Spirituality Intuition
Pure blue	Religious feeling Truth
Blue, tipped with lavender	Devotion Noble ideals Peace Music

Blue, mixed with dark
  radiations
	Selfish religious
	  feelings

Blue, mixed with grey	Religious feeling plus fear

Green	Adaptability
	Balance
	Equilibrium
	Evolution
	Development
Light green	Sympathy
Green, mixed with red-brown, or with murky red	Jealousy
Dirty, muddy green	Low deceit
	Cunning
	Falsehood
	Trickery
Green, with light grey	Deceit
Indigo	Royalty
Violet	Devotion
	Ceremonial tendencies
	Tendencies toward ritual
	Vitality
	Organization
	Harmony
Purple	Spiritual love
	Sacrifice
Lavender	High spirituality
Lilac	Love for humanity

Pale grey	Fear
	Horror
Dark grey, mixed with brownish red	Depression
	Pessimism
Greenish, reddish brown	Selfishness
Reddish brown	Avarice
	Greed
Black	Negation of spiritual value
	Crime
	Denial
	Pollution
	Sickness
	Malice
	Hatred
	Revenge
White	Holiness
	Purity
	Innocence
	Self
	Contact with Shamballa

Dominating Colors

Red	Artist
Orange	Co-worker, helper
Yellow	Philosopher, aspirant of wisdom
Green	Helper and healer, true doctor
Blue	Mystic, aspirant
Violet	Priest, Initiate
Purple	Elder Brother

Primary Colors: Red, yellow, blue

Secondary Colors:

Yellow plus blue	Green
Yellow plus red	Orange
Blue plus red	Purple
Blue plus green plus orange plus purple	Indigo

All other colors may be formed by the addition of white or black.

Chapter 7

Diversification of the Aura

The auras of people differ from each other in many ways. There are

1. oval auras
2. balloon auras
3. dislocated auras
4. diffused auras
5. dirty or chaotic auras
6. separated auras
7. loose auras
8. cracked auras
9. obsessed auras
10. pinched auras
11. contagious auras

12. radiant auras

13. dynamic auras

14. group auras

15. auras blended with the Master

16. overshadowing auras

17. mixed auras

18. crystallized or frozen auras

1. The oval aura is the natural aura, one to eight feet around the body.

2. The balloon aura is when a part of the aura hangs like a balloon around the head or at the sides. This is caused by abstract dreaming and spaced mental states. The person feels that a part of himself is not anchored in the brain or in the body. This aura is also one of the main causes of epilepsy.

3. The dislocated aura has a part of the aura which is not in its right place. For example, the mental aura is normally around the head, extending to the shoulders. It is considered dislocated when it is found on the solar plexus or sacral center.

The causes of dislocation are many. An accident can pull the mental body down to the location of the injury, and the intense pain keeps it there. This is what causes a person to pass out. It also causes various mental disturbances.

Dislocation sometimes occurs slowly, when continuous attention is given to certain locations, such as the stomach or sex organs. Sometimes the mental body corrects itself; sometimes it cannot. In the latter case, the man falls into addiction.

Fear can dislocate parts of the aura, permanently or temporarily. Dislocation happens when one loses something or someone dear to him. Sometimes the wrong kinds of sexual relationships can dislocate the aura, such as oral sex or homosexual relationships.

Each time dislocation occurs, a person comes closer to losing his stability. Many mental conditions originate from dislocation of the aura. This condition affects logic, creates confusion, light-headedness, absentmindedness, and insanity. The use of drugs, marijuana, excessive sex, and alcohol contribute greatly to the dislocation of the aura.

Dislocation of the etheric body contributes to heart attacks, strokes, paralysis, and heavy depression. When a part of the aura is condensed and accumulated in certain places, that location receives seventy to eighty percent more energy than the usual amount. This energy creates tumors, cancers, and other degenerative diseases.

It is observed that the population of certain cities have auras that are swollen in the same way. This is one of the main reasons why there is so much disease related to both male and female sex organs in certain areas. The first effect of congestion is a feeling of over-stimulation. Then, because the organs cannot handle the presence of the voltage, they take unnatural measures to protect themselves, and they swell or crack.

Those who are over-occupied with sex and commit various crimes to achieve satisfaction have auras which are swollen near their generative organs.

4. A diffused aura is one in which the colors and geometric formations are in a nebulous condition. The mental and emotional lives of such people are characterized by uncertainty, confusion, lack of interest, and inertia. These people can be drawn in any direction and can be used for any crime when enough force is given to them. Such people live in a sphere of total goallessness.

5. There are distinct colors and geometric lines in a dirty or chaotic aura, but they are in ever-changing motion in which one cannot see any recognizable patterns. Colors mix and disappear, then return in different locations and form different mixtures in which there is no harmony. If one could hear this chaotic condition, it would sound like inharmonious noise and random cacophony.

6. A separated aura occurs when the mental and astral bodies look separated from the body. This is a warning that the person is going to die very soon. Such a condition also occurs under the pressure of heavy guilt feelings, crime, self-rejection, or a determination to commit suicide. A separated aura also occurs before an accident which you can tell will occur or in a moment of great horror.

Sometimes instead of separation the aura contracts and disappears into the body, causing heavy pressure upon the heart, kidneys, ovaries, testes, and brain. High blood pressure is the direct result of such a condition. Some heart attacks are the result of a sudden withdrawal or separation of the aura. In painful accidents, a person passes out to save the body from heavy pain. Passing out also is one of the results of a separated aura.

Separated auras are very common in places where explosions occur. The bombing of cities and the shelling of armies create auric separations. In times of great danger, the aura also separates from the body.

Sometimes if the aura separates many times, it creates acute mental problems — even total insanity. Separation can last a few minutes, a few hours, or it can become chronic, meaning that it happens periodically when past memories are repeatedly restimulated.

Sometimes dislocation in the emotional or mental bodies continues in the subtle and fiery worlds. The human soul is the center of the aura, but loses this central position because of dislocation and separation of the aura. The aura is still tied to the human soul by the life thread in this instance.

Partial separation of the aura occurs if the person has developed his various bodies. For example, a person can take his mental body and travel to a far-distant land for a special service. A clairvoyant would see the absence of the mental aura from around the body, which may return shortly after the labor has been completed.

Our vehicles can be used by the Inner Guide on special occasions, often without our conscious awareness. During these times, the body feels tired. During such an experience, it is suggested that the person remain silent and relax until the vehicle is returned to his body. On such occasions, the mental body is usually used.

The absence of the emotional body is also observed when a person is in a state of great admiration, worship, or identification with certain objects. The emotional body momentarily detaches from the body and fuses with the object of admiration, worship, or identification.

Dislocated or separated auras create a great hindrance to the evolution of the human soul. Fear is a great contributor to the separation of the aura. Unfortunately, fear techniques are prevalent at this time. Governments use them to a large degree. Insurance companies, physicians, psychiatrists, educators, ministers, and tax collectors all apply fear techniques at every opportunity, creating a generation of insane people.

Fear techniques must be entirely eliminated if we want a healthy world for ourselves and for generations to come. Unfortunately, people think that fear makes money for them, that fear makes people obey the law, that fear "inspires" people to inherit the Kingdom of God. But the whole world is suffering under the darkness of fear. Any time a person feels, acts, speaks, thinks, plans, or makes love because of fear, he not only creates poison within his system, but he also spreads that poison in space, like the pollution that spreads from a factory smokestack.

7. A loose aura is one which fluctuates in and out, creating great waves of instability in the mind, emotions, and health.

8. A cracked aura is very dangerous. Cracks occur when the circumference of the astral aura breaks and the mental aura flows into the astral aura, or vice versa. It also happens that the astral aura flows into the etheric aura.

A cracked aura puts the person in contact with astral, mental, or etheric entities who misuse him and make his life miserable. If a cracked aura absorbs the energy of higher planes, the centers and corresponding organs of the cracked vehicle are burned. Brain tumors and various degenerative diseases are a direct result of an influx of energy for which the physical vehicle is not ready.

A cracked aura also transmits a great amount of energy to those around, giving others the impression that the person is charged with superhuman force. Most criminals have this great amount of force, which floods their life and charges other human beings. Hitler is one example of a person whose force organized his immediate followers and the masses and led his country to destruction.

9. An obsessed aura is a very unhealthy condition in which many astral and etheric entities come and dwell in the aura. They not only create a split personality, confusion, and tension, but they also take over the lower

centers and use them for excessive sex, crime, slander, malice, and destruction. Most obsessed people end their lives in suicide.

Obsessing entities are of various kinds:

- spirits living in etheric realms, earthbound ones who seek to possess you in order to contact the physical world
- spirits of those to whom you were unrighteous, criminal, or destructive
- wives or husbands whom you betrayed by your actions
- dark forces that hate your progress and are able to enter your aura because of your various weaknesses
- low-level nature spirits, who like stagnated auras. Mediums, channels and lower psychics are sources of such kinds of contamination.

10. A pinched aura is a wounded aura. This kind of aura comes into being as a result of psychic attacks or the bad thoughts and emotions of people directed toward you.

Bad thoughts often pierce your aura like nails piercing wood. Negative emotions create "warts" in your aura. Psychic attacks from dark forces create rents in your aura. But those who are shielded with strong determination to serve others can repel such attacks.

11. A contagious aura is one filled with hatred, malice, fear, anger, greed, jealousy, and revenge. These emotions have specific colors and formations. Those who come close to such an aura absorb its pollution into their aura and contaminate it.

12. A radiant aura is the healthiest aura through which the unfolding human soul radiates, creating geometrical configurations in the aura and splendid colors. A radiant aura spreads joy, enthusiasm, and inspiration. Like sunshine, it brings life to people within its sphere of influence and leads them toward success, achievement, service, and creativity.

A radiant aura develops after one has passed the first initiation. The first initiation is the birth of the human soul, when the light of the human soul radiates out of the periphery of the aura, energizing and stimulating the etheric centers. Radiation increases as the person steps into greater stages of initiation. His light shines out until the Third Initiation, when his total aura becomes transfigured and he reaches the stage of Transfiguration. At the Fifth Initiation, he radiates twelve rays, which gradually bring him into contact with the heart center of the Solar Logos.

It is interesting to note that in the first initiation there are three radiations, or rays. In the second initiation, there are five. In the Third Initiation, there are seven. In the Fourth Initiation, there are nine. In the Fifth Initiation, there are twelve.

When the aura is radioactive, it contains three elements: joy, beauty, and harmony. All healing is the result of joy, beauty, and harmony. Those who develop their aura shine out as natural healers and benefactors of humanity.

13. A dynamic aura is a highly energized aura, due to fiery streams of energy coming from higher ethers or centers. Such an aura spreads enthusiasm, love, and energy and keeps groups and organizations in continuous labor for the service of humanity.

14. The group aura is a phenomenon that appears in individuals who have very close relations with their family members or group members. No matter how far the individuals are from each other, their auras reflect the auras of the other members of the family or group. When they are together, all their auras blend and fuse.

Such auric formations provide a great help to the Hierarchy because through such groups the Great Ones can safely transmit Their energies to the world. The group aura is possible only when there is total love and an absence of criticism.

15. An aura blended with the Master is achieved when one pays all his karmic debts and sanctifies his life for the service of the Hierarchy. A portion of the Master's intuitive and atmic aura comes and fuses itself with your aura and becomes a permanent station of contact with the Master. In this relationship, the disciple lives and works only for the plan of his Master; all his expressions are performed in the light of his Master's presence.

16. An overshadowing aura is a part of the aura of a Great One which is sent to you as a rain cloud of spiritual inspiration. This is located above your head and continuously transmits great ideas, visions, wisdom, and revelations to your head or heart center and prepares you for a great responsibility. The overshadowing aura guides and protects you and helps you fulfill your mission. It gradually becomes a transmitting station between you and your Teacher.

Overshadowing happens at a time of great crisis. Joan of Arc was overshadowed to fulfill a dangerous mission. We are told that both Roosevelt and Churchill were overshadowed during World War II. Martin Luther King, Gandhi, and many others throughout history have been overshadowed.

17. A mixed aura comes into existence when through sexual intercourse two auras mix and blend, and parts of each aura are absorbed into the other.

Advanced clairvoyants can see in your aura the image of the one with whom you have had sex. Sometimes such a relation advances your evolution; sometimes it retards it, according to the level and karmic accumulations of your partner.

18. A crystallized or frozen aura is like a swimming pool in which ice formation takes place. In certain conditions the human aura crystallizes, and there are patches of the aura floating in certain parts of the aura or they become stationary.

Dogma, doctrine, prejudice, fanaticism, and superstition create crystallizations in the aura. These crystallizations prevent the free circulation of energy in the aura, and they deteriorate the glands and organs in the body. Petrification or atrophy of certain glands is the direct reflection of crystallized patches in the aura.

Crystallized portions of the aura look like callouses which cannot receive or transmit energy. They are dead parts of the aura which eventually come together and form a large blockage in the aura. Certain malfunctions of organs or painful attacks of disease are the direct result of such accumulated crystallizations.

It is important to know that joy, gratitude, tolerance, solemnity, honesty, nobility, and courage make our auras beautiful. The ancients used to say that a beautiful aura is a magnet for inspiration and energy.

Chapter 8

Petrification of the Aura

Petrification of the aura is a reality. Our seven centers in the etheric, astral, and mental bodies work upon seven principles. For example, the head center lives through the principle of purpose. The heart center through the principle of compassion. The throat center lives through contact with the principle of rhythm in the Universe. The ajna center nourishes itself upon the energy it directs. The solar plexus lives through the principle of peace and harmony. The sacral center lives through the principle of creativity. The base of spine center lives through the principle of will energy.

If we violate any principle in any way with our actions, emotions, or thoughts, we create petrification. Petrification is a phenomenon in which the elements of the same center create positive and negative polarizations which block each other and create inertia. For example, any action against compassion causes a certain amount of petrification around the heart center and circulatory system.

Every time we misuse the power of creativity, we create petrification in our sacral center. Every time we work or live against the fundamental purpose of our soul, we cause petrification in the head center and in the corresponding pineal gland. When petrification advances, the centers cannot pump energy, and their corresponding organs or systems degenerate.

Petrification in the aura appears like dry paint. When the aura is coated with many layers of petrification, the person's contact with the Universe is cut, and he becomes selfish, self-seeking, and criminal.

Our aura is a sensitive instrument as a whole, which keeps us in harmony with the life of the Universe. When the aura is petrified, an individual loses his direction, his balance and stability, and prepares himself for decay.

Just as the aura of a person can become petrified to a greater or lesser extent, the aura of a nation or group can petrify, resulting in inertia, depression, and chaos. Exploitation in national life, heavy taxation, and violation of freedom are senseless effects of petrification. When petrification advances, ruling bodies lose their sanity and direction and try to sap their own people to survive.

Petrification is the result of a reaction originated by the principle. Reaction to thoughts, emotions, words, and deeds creates conflict in the centers. Conflict weakens the centers and leads them into inertia and petrification. For example, the principle of the heart is compassion or inclusiveness. When you think, speak, or act against this principle, your heart reacts and tries to reject or refuse those thoughts, words, or actions.

In the moment of rejection, the two energies — the principle and the reaction to the principle — clash, and your heart center receives a harmful shock. If these shocks are repeated, you dig your own grave.

We must remember that the main principle behind the above-mentioned seven principles is the Self, the Divine Presence which stands for the One Self and for Beauty, Goodness, Righteousness, Joy, Freedom, Striving, and Sacrificial Service.

Petrification of a center prevents energy from reaching its corresponding gland or organ. Whenever the flow of energy decreases, the organ grows out of proportion in reaching for more energy. But as much as it grows, the available energy provides less and less, and the organ eventually collapses. Enlargement of organs is a sign of their impending destruction.

Petrified locations of the human aura must be loosened if one wants to restore his health. The increase of crystallizations in the aura is responsible for most of our health, moral, and social problems.

Imagine the aura as a pool of water in which you can see pieces of floating ice — the petrified spots in the aura. Sometimes it happens that through identical vibration, these petrified spots are drawn to each other to form a larger crystal. Because of the factor of a common denominator, sometimes all of the pieces suddenly unite and form a layer of ice over the entire surface of the aura. This is a very dangerous condition which leads to total inertia, depression, and suicide. The same thing can happen to the aura of a group or nation.

There are also anti-crystallization elements in our being. For example, a strong decision to live a beautiful life stands as a fiery breaker of crystallizations. Our aspirations, past good deeds, memories of heroic images, love of beauty and compassion, solemnity, goodwill, and so on are all elements in our aura which prevent certain crystallizations.

Our Inner Guide sometimes recharges us, restoring the currents of electricity within our being. Sometimes our Teacher or a friendly spirit can recharge our system and give us a chance to overcome our crystallizations or petrifications.

Sometimes certain inspirations act as rechargers. These inspirations are received through enjoying beauty, a creative book, an enlightening lecture, or uplifting music.

There are also diamonds and pearls of bliss in our aura. The pearls are formed through our best thoughts, words, and deeds. The diamonds are our heroic actions and deeds. These jewels remain in our aura and work to keep the flow and circulation in our aura continuous by attacking and melting away any kind of crystallization, bringing restoration to the centers, glands, and organs.

When we increase these treasures in our aura, they form a protective garland. A great Initiate shines and radiates beautiful fragrance in space. In the Ageless Wisdom we are advised to collect the jewels of bliss and wisdom. These are the candles which will shine on our path to Infinity. Unification of diamonds and pearls creates moments of ecstasy, inspiration, and resurrection.

It is good to have joyful, enthusiastic, and freedom-loving friends around us. They act to recharge us; their presence can prevent crystallizations from forming. Joy and enthusiasm are fiery elements which heal, purify, and uplift. Conversely, one must be careful in catering to depressed or negative friends, as they increase one's petrification.

The main contributors to the petrification of the aura are

1. images and memories of failure
2. rejection
3. hatred
4. fanaticism
5. vanity
6. resentment
7. separatism

1. **Accumulated images, experiences, or memories of failure** collectively form a crystallization in the aura. Images, memories, and experiences of success and achievement build the protective nets of diamonds and pearls within us.

2. **Rejection** creates crystallization. One must be very careful about accepting or rejecting things. Rejection must always be carried out in such a way that a negative image is not formed in the mind of the person who is rejected. When a person is forcefully rejected, when a race is rejected, and so on, they develop petrification in their aura which acts as a transmitter of destructive forces. One can produce an army against himself by living in an attitude of rejection.

We are advised in the literature of the Ageless Wisdom to be very careful about our expectations so as not to be disappointed by rejection. In some schools, Teachers advise the cultivation of intelligent passivity to free oneself from the attacks of rejection.

The idea of rejection needs a little explanation so as not to mislead our thinking. For example, if a wealthy man approaches you and asks for your jacket, shoes, and shirt, you are not rejecting him or creating crystallization in his aura if you say, "No." There is a principle of righteousness in the Universe. Only when you break this principle do you create rejection. Sometimes your intellect cannot discriminate between righteousness and unrighteousness, but the principle of righteousness acts and refuses without creating the effect of rejection.

Real rejection is an act against the principle of righteousness. For example, a woman has an illegitimate child and she asks for financial help from the father, but he rejects her. This creates crystallization in his aura and in hers. The woman can protect herself from crystallization by thinking that perhaps her situation is karmic and that is what is producing the rejection. But this will not work on the man's behalf because the principle of righteousness immediately produces crystallization in him, no matter upon what grounds he bases his rejection to help her.

3. **Hatred** crystallizes the aura. It can be like an epidemic, spreading itself into the hearts of the multitudes and petrifying the heart centers of the people. Hatred is seen in the aura as a black-brown patch of color with red spots.

Every moment of hatred produces the substance of crystallization, which becomes the originating source of our many troubles and diseases.

4. **Fanaticism** brings a major crystallization within the mental and emotional bodies. This crystallization blocks the heart and head centers; the person loses his guidance and compassion and engages in criminal actions.

Fanaticism lives by the energy of will power derived from the sacral center and is sustained by the life-energy flowing in the etheric and physical bodies.

It is not surprising that religious and spiritual groups develop fanaticism and act exactly opposite to the principles of love, light, and freedom. Fanaticism is symbolized by a rattlesnake that dies from a self-inflicted bite. Fanaticism appears in the aura like a black cloud with muddy green and red pins around and in the formation. Fanaticism creates acidification in many organs.

5. **Vanity** builds a false image in the aura which, not being a natural part of the constitution of the system, floats like an iceberg in the aura, causing certain disturbances. When vanity is fed continuously, it gradually sends out roots and establishes itself as a permanent resident in the aura, eventually becoming a ruling factor in the life of the person.

Vanity obscures reality, and the person develops a tendency to escape from reality, from facts, and live in the image of his vanity. Vanity distorts the impressions and inspirations coming from space. If we keep our aura free from vanity, we will be in better contact with the guiding and healing forces of Nature.

6. **Resentment** is a major factor in the crystallization process. To prevent such a process, one must develop contentment and the spirit of gratitude. The spirit of gratitude is a great solvent which dissolves many kinds of crystallizations in the aura and restores health.

7. **Separatism** acts against the greatest principle and law in the Universe — unity. Every separative thought, word, expression, action, or intention creates crystallization in the aura and even builds walls around the subtle bodies. When a person passes away in such a condition, he cannot communicate with the life of the Subtle Worlds; he resembles a cocoon thrown into the ocean.

Separative people reject the life-giving energies of the Universe. They reject expansion, synthesis, and unity, and they turn into tumors in the body of the Universe.

Separatism is an anti-survival factor which, by all means, must be dissolved before it gains strength.

Every kind of sickness we have in our physical body has its counterpart or correspondence in our emotional and mental bodies. For example, ulcers are jealousy in the emotional body and worry in the mental body. It would be wonderful to heal these three manifestations simultaneously because if only one of them is healed, the others reproduce the same problem over and over again.

It would be very interesting to conduct extensive research regarding the emotional and mental conditions that people have at the time of certain diseases in an attempt to trace the cause of their diseases to the subtler bodies.

When we damage our astral or mental body, we carry with us a defective body to the Subtle Worlds. This is why one must not only try to make his physical body really healthy and beautiful for his relatively short duration on earth, but also perfect and sublimate his subtle bodies for the much longer duration spent in the Subtle Worlds.

In the astral body the major sicknesses are hatred, jealousy, fear, anger, greed, depression, and revenge. They are first-degree killers, corresponding to the diseases of the body which are prevalent today.

In the mental body the major sicknesses are grief, separatism, vanity, pride, fanaticism, hypocrisy, superstition, and prejudice. At this time these sicknesses are the roots of many physical and social problems.

Habits are etheric sicknesses. Addictions are again etheric sicknesses, which provide a vast field of interesting problems for humanity.

The germs or microbes that exist in our body are actually the vehicles of real germs and microbes that exist in our aura. Germs get their start in the aura, or they are imported by our aura. In the aura, they seek nourishment; they multiply and then attack the physical body. The best conditions for multiplication of germs in the aura are depression, anger, fear, hatred, jealousy, and revenge. It is true that before your body is contaminated by germs, your aura is first contaminated. The germs of contagious diseases do not travel from one physical body to another, but from one aura to another.

If a person is sick and your aura is radioactive, you do not catch his germs through touch. The aura imports the germs and kills them, or multiplies them and then passes them on to the physical body. If, in certain cases, direct contamination takes place between two physical bodies or because medical tools have transplanted the contamination from one body to another, the organ is not affected until its counterpart in the aura is defeated by the germs.

Enthusiasm, love, gratitude, lofty thoughts, and a spirit of sacrificial service create electrification in the aura, which can burn and destroy many attacks. Actually, the aura is a multidimensional field where the major battle of our life goes on.

Sicknesses in the aura have different formations. For example, greed resembles an octopus and floats within the aura. It sticks its arms in the aura of other persons close to it. Jealousy is like a fiery red-black worm that eats the aura. Hatred is like a poisonous fume coming from underground. Fear is like an acid mist which spreads on the nerve channels and accumulates in the kidneys.

Glamors and negative emotions petrify parts of the emotional aura. Thoughtforms of illusions, fanaticism, and vanity petrify the mental aura and form callouses on it. In these cases, the aura cannot expand regularly, and canyons or walls come into being in our aura.

The etheric body crystallizes by accumulating maya. Maya is the urge and drive accumulated by hypnotic suggestions or techniques of over-stimulation. Maya is mostly related to sex and food.

When the etheric body crystallizes, the body loses control over its weight, and obesity is the result. To keep the etheric body in good shape, one must exercise deep breathing and heavy labor and avoid fattening foods, starch, sugar, and liquor.

Crystallization of the aura blocks the function of the centers and affects the lymphatic system and glands. The circulatory system in the body is controlled by the etheric body.

The following is a list of the primary poisons which hurt the aura:

— sneakiness
— lying
— hypocrisy
— selfishness
— separatism
— disobedience to the rules of ethics
— stealing
— gossip
— malice
— slander
— wrong sexual relations
— hatred

We know that the state of consciousness affects the aura, and through the aura, the physical body. But the reverse is also true. When a person changes his aura through outer influences, not only the health of the body is affected, but various changes also occur in his state of consciousness. It is not the aura which directly affects the physical body, but it is the changes of consciousness that deeply affect the body through the etheric body.

Noises created by airplanes or machines, radio waves, radioactivity, microwaves, electrical currents, batteries, magnets, and so on have a very strong effect on the aura. They can

• contract the aura

- create cracks in the aura
- sap the vitality of the aura
- create dislocations in the aura
- create cleavages between the glands, centers, and auric flows
- affect the consciousness

Sound, audible or inaudible, has a very powerful effect on the aura. Sound may destroy the aura and decompose it; if handled properly, it can purify the aura.

Odors and decaying bodies or materials affect the aura. Animal emanations have a bad effect on the human aura, especially the emanations of dogs. Stagnant water, polluted air, and certain plants, for example, poison oak, can cause great damage to the aura.

On the other hand, eucalyptus, pine, and oak trees have a very soothing effect on the aura. They transmit psychic energy, which is very beneficent for the aura.

Negative emotions burn the aura, especially in the area of the solar plexus and the knees. Burned auras use the salts of the body, weaken it, and bring in many complications.

Thoughts based on hatred, fear, anger, greed, jealousy, and separatism darken the mental aura and hinder the energy transmitted through the mental aura to the etheric and physical bodies. It is the energy transmitted by the mental body that assimilates the prana of the air through the spleen and etheric triangle.

At sunrise our aura inhales the vitality of the sun. At sunset it exhales and relaxes, if no emotions or thoughts keep it in irritation. Meditation expands and purifies the aura. Worry, anxieties, and depression are like strong poisons for the aura.

Chapter 9

Transformation of the Aura

In our aura we have the etheric body, which has four levels. The higher we go, the more refined each layer is. Then we have the astral aura and two mental auras, lower and higher. Corresponding to these four auras, we have the Intuitional aura, the Atmic, Monadic, and Divine auras, if they are developed. These four are called the four Cosmic Ethers or the higher ethers.

A healthy aura has ever-flowing electrical currents traveling through it in parallel fashion, as well as a more mysterious movement whereby certain atoms from the lower ethers, or etheric body, move up to the next higher level of that body, or to the astral, mental, or even Intuitional aura, changing their color and intensity from one level to another. In the meantime, certain atoms are discarded to the periphery of the aura to be burned or dumped into the atmosphere. These are "dead" atoms which the bodies can no longer use.

This process continues until the higher ethers eventually penetrate to the lower ethers and finally transmute them into higher ethers. Similar activities occur between the astral and mental bodies and higher bodies — the Intuitional, Atmic, Monadic, and Divine bodies. Age after age, this process of transmutation continues until the aura turns into a glorious rainbow. This is the "perfection" which every human being must one day reach.

How does this transformation start? It starts through

1. aspiration toward beauty
2. meditation
3. evening review
4. trying to live a life of beauty, goodness, righteousness, and freedom, for the good of the whole world
5. joy
6. retreats
7. intense creativity
8. prayer
9. direct contact with the Teacher

If people try to follow this ninefold path, they will gradually transmute their auras and enjoy health, expand their consciousness, and become highly creative leaders in humanity.

1. **Aspiration** is an intense striving toward beauty in all forms.

2. **Meditation** causes radioactivity in the atoms of the lower bodies and urges them to travel to the higher bodies.

3. **Evening review** clears the tape of impressions and creates harmony in the aura.[1]

4. **Trying to live according to the standards of beauty, goodness, righteousness, and freedom** nourishes the striving atoms so that they can continue their path toward greater light.

5. **Joy** attracts energy from the Higher Self into the aura.

6. **Retreats** cause stabilization in the aura.

7. **Intense creativity** brings higher streams of energy into the aura.

8. **Prayer** creates contact with Higher Forces.

9. **Direct contact with the Teacher** causes intense mobilization of atoms to travel to higher planes.

The goal is to reach the Inner Glory and radiate It out to the world of slavery and misery.

Meditation draws higher substance from the higher mental and intuitional levels and transmits it to the lower bodies, thus causing regeneration and transmutation in them. It even changes one's facial complexion. Take a clear picture of yourself before you start meditation,

---

1. See Ch. 80, "Evening Review," in *The Psyche and Psychism.*

and then six months later take another picture; you will see the changes. Continuous meditation refines the body and makes it more beautiful. It especially changes the eyes and face, pouring more refined and lively atoms into your aura.

You can find out if certain foods, sexual practices, drugs, marijuana, or alcohol are disturbing your aura by conducting the following tests:

1. Put a sentence on the wall and see from how many feet back you can read it. Mark the distance. Then try to read the same sentence from that distance after using alcohol, or drugs, and so on. If you must step closer to read the sentence, it is a sign that you are disturbing your aura by participating in these practices.

2. Stand on your right foot with the left foot on top of the right. If you shake and cannot stand still, you are in some way damaging your aura and related bodies.

3. Hold your hand out in front of you and stretch your fingers apart. If you cannot hold your hand in this position without your hand trembling or moving, you are somehow damaging your aura.

You may try these three tests one hour after intercourse. If you are shaky or cannot read the sentence at the original distance, you can be sure of three things:

    a. the person you had relations with is sapping you

    b. you are exaggerating your sexual activities

c. your aura is in disturbance

However, you cannot reach a valid conclusion if you do not test yourself at least a few times.

Another test that you can do after intercourse is to try to thread a very small needle. You can also close your eyes and try to walk a straight line. By observing yourself closely, you will soon come to know what to do and what not to do.

My Teacher once said that the power of a speaker or lecturer lies not in his words but in his aura. In order to have a powerful, coordinated, and harmonious aura, he said that one must abstain from sex for a few days before the lecture and stay away from drugs, alcohol, marijuana, coffee, and black tea.

He was a very dynamic speaker. He and his wife lived ten miles from the monastery, but three days before giving a seminar, he would come and stay in the monastery as a retreat. He radiated light, joy, and energy.

A similar practice is followed by Armenian priests who are married. They stay in the parish house on Friday and Saturday nights and abstain from relations with their wives in order to focus their souls on the service they will render Sunday morning. We are told that the auras of such people include the whole audience and transmit higher blessings to all who are present.

No matter how lofty is the philosophy or psychology that a speaker uses to influence his audience, if his aura is not energetic and radiant he cannot create changes in the audience; sometimes he even creates rejection in the audience. The aura amplifies your words and impresses them in the auras of others before your words even reach their ears, which are often occupied with other interferences.

During the three-to seven-day period of the full moon, one must abstain from sex if he wants to strengthen and organize his aura. The best way to distort the aura is to practice oral sex, or to have intercourse with a woman during her period.

The following four steps are recommended by great Teachers. They say that in order to make our aura more radioactive we need to

— eat proper food and sometimes fast to help cleanse physical impurities

— increase our love, compassion, and kindness

— think harmlessly and concentrate the mind upon objects of devotion and dedication

— express joy, gratitude, and patience

Also, if you meditate for six months on each of the following seed thoughts, you can build a very beautiful aura. Along with meditation, however, you must try to put these ideas into practice, write about them, and teach them to others:

• Striving

• Daring

• Courage

- Solemnity
- Gratitude
- Perseverance
- Discrimination
- Sense of Responsibility
- Fearlessness
- Patience
- Compassion
- Enthusiasm

The term "discrimination" is used to mean the ability to choose between those things which help you progress in light and those things which prevent you from advancing in light.

Of course, by looking at this list you will be able to see how many years it will take to complete all twelve seed thoughts. Some people think, "In this amount of time, I could learn a profession and make more money instead." But without a healthy aura, one will enjoy neither his money nor his position. Besides, all it takes is fifteen minutes to half an hour each day to meditate. If a person spent fifteen minutes each day meditating on one of the twelve virtues for six months, it totals approximately six days of eight-hour days. Can't we "sacrifice" six days in six months to make our lives more beautiful and glorious?

Chapter 10

Friction in the Aura

All your states of consciousness, emotions, activities, thoughts, urges, and drives reflect in the aura — which means that they influence your health, expressions, the way you live, your creativity, and your relationships.

Conflict starts when two forces have different frequencies which cannot be harmonized. For example, you have learned that lying is not good, but you lie. Now two opposite forces are created in you, and they are in conflict. Conflict exhausts your energy and leads to sickness and insanity.

You can settle the conflict in favor of the principle or the lie. For example, you can refuse to admit that you lied. The frequencies in you which are built by thoughts to help others interfere and end the conflict on the surface, but the conflict goes on and creates cleavages because by supporting the lie, you defeat or deny the Self and increase Its enemies.

But if you settle the conflict on behalf of the Self, you advance. How can you settle for the Self? You can think, for example, "Let me go and confess, and pay for the damage I have done." You do not ignore the higher principle, but strengthen it. The lower nature may not like this, but it cannot hurt you and the conflict is settled.

Conflict creates

- whirlpools, which are very dangerous
- cleavages between auras and hardening edges
- cracks through which the higher fire burns the lower

In a healthy aura the colors fuse and blend like a rainbow; they nourish and serve each other. When the colors are sharp-edged, this indicates problems in the aura.

The aura is like a "sticky" mist. It sticks to anything you touch. Before you physically touch something, the aura touches it. But the aura does not stick unless the fire emanated by the touch makes it stick. Money carries a lot of auric substance. It must be blessed or cleansed under the fire of thought. Auric patches which are stuck to any object may be transmitted to you if you touch that object. Books which have not been previously used carry the aura of the author. Used books carry a lot of auric "feathers" around them. If music is played by the composer, it carries his energy. If it is played by others, it is mixed.

What you build in others is what you become. The influence you have on others determines your state of beingness in the future. In other words, you build yourself with the hands of others, according to the blueprint you have given them. This plan is the impression you make on them in the relationships you have with them.

The aura is not only substance but also color. Beyond the Intuitional Plane, it is sound. On higher planes, it is active energy if it is pure. If it is not pure, it is a polluting stream in space.

Great Ones and astral and mental entities watch you and hear you. Your life is like a movie to them.

The aura can be developed and stabilized using the following aids:

1. silence
2. solitude
3. rest
4. good thoughts
5. gratitude
6. spiritual striving
7. meditation
8. periodic abstinence from sex
9. natural oils such as
   - musk
   - eucalyptus
   - rose oil
   - pine oil
   - bay leaf oil

- cassia
- peppermint
10. short periods of exposure to sunshine
11. pure relationships
12. inner peace
13. creativity
14. joy

Silence is very beneficial to the aura. Any time you feel tired, negative, or exhausted, exercise silence. Go to the mountains, the ocean, or the desert and spend a few days or weeks there. Canyons or caves are the best places for rest and silence, as there are less electronic waves in such places. Try not to have any noise around you, except for the sounds of waterfalls, waves, or the wind through the trees.

Silence heals and invigorates the aura. You can keep silence emotionally and mentally, relaxing your actions and internal conversations. Mental and emotional silence have a great restorative effect on the aura.

Too much talking wastes a tremendous amount of substance from the aura, and if the speech is not of high quality, full of gossip, criticism, and slander, it burns precious parts of the aura.

Relaxation is a very important factor in curing and energizing the aura.[1] Also learn how to relax your emo-

---

1. See also pp. 79-80 in *The Science of Meditation* for a daily exercise on relaxation.

tional and mental auras. Your aura is like your muscles. When you learn to sense it, you can learn how to relax it.

Whenever you are excited, angry, emotionally irritated, or mentally agitated, relax your emotional and mental bodies for ten to fifteen minutes, releasing all agitation from the aura. You can learn to do this through practice. Do not use any mechanical methods. Gently use your will, and you will be amazed at the results.

Generally, physical relaxation helps emotional and mental relaxation. Relaxation of the aura gives a chance for the creative forces in your nature to penetrate the damaged parts of the aura and heal them.

Sleeping is a great way to relax the physical body, but it is not effective for the emotional or mental bodies, except when you relax them before going to sleep. Deeper sleep is not yet known to the average human being. Deeper sleep is withdrawal from the astral and mental bodies, entering the sanctuary of silence — the Intuitional body. Those who can enter there can heal themselves, if karma allows them to be healed.

We are told in the Teaching that our aura can act as a shield in various conditions. For example, perhaps in a past life we killed people or hurt them extensively in many ways. When we meet these people in this life, some hostile force emanates from them toward us, and they unconsciously hate us, reject us, and feel like damaging us. Many hostilities which apparently have no reason are deeply rooted in the past. In such conditions, we can avoid the hostile force only by having a purified and well-developed aura, which immediately acts against these forces and breaks their intensity, or even returns them to their source. Many poisonous arrows are deflected by the aura.

The Teaching emphasizes the necessity of organizing and purifying the aura through the energy of love and pure thoughts. A purified and developed aura increases the love in others; they act in your favor and feel joy in helping you. A purified and highly organized aura can sometimes protect a group of people from negative attacks or from hostilities which originated in past lives. It is also possible that a beautiful aura can protect the aura of a close friend who is under attack.

The aura acts automatically against such attacks, while the person is usually totally unconscious of his reactions. Rays are found within the aura which have the ability to detect certain attacks. These rays originate in the Chalice and bypass the brain.

The aura also reacts in a similar way to any attack coming from the astral or etheric plane. There may be people who were damaged, hurt, or killed by us because of our duties, position, or by accident. These people may harbor a great deal of revenge or negative feelings against us, and they very often try to obsess or possess us to satisfy those feelings. But if our aura is highly developed and purified, it becomes almost impossible for them even to make an attempt to possess us because our aura hits them with an electric shock. It is only when the aura is weakened that they have a chance to penetrate.

It is known that in the presence of certain individuals, people do not experience any psychic attack. Such individuals are sometimes referred to as "Towers." It is true that Towers are attacked by many arrows, but they fall by the wayside after hitting solid rock.

We are told that a golden-red light sometimes appears in the aura. This is called the "armor of the heart." It is this light which destroys the attacks of the dark forces in the subtle planes. The strongest and most powerful weapon against the dark forces is the golden-red light of the heart because it radiates the fire of life. We are told that the bodies of the dark forces consist of etheric, astral, and lower mental substance, and this substance cannot withstand the heat of the fire of the heart.

If the heart glows, the psychic attacks of the dark forces can come no closer than three feet. Often the light of the heart hits the attacker like an electrical shock and repels him. After each shock, the aura of the person gains in strength. Thus, the opposition evokes greater resources into action.

In the aura, the heart plays the greatest role. Golden-red light is an electrical flame which ever stands on guard.

Chapter 11

The Virtues and Vices

Virtues and vices are the fruits of the same energy, either used in an involutionary way or an evolutionary way.

Every vice can change to its corresponding virtue if the energy behind the vice is used on the arc of evolution.

Vices or virtues condition the color of our aura. Dull, muddy, pale, or grey auras indicate vices, while translucent, clear, strong, and florescent auras indicate virtues.

As the virtues involve the threefold personality, the aura becomes more glorious, and its radiation and magnetism increases with its healing, enlightening, and strengthening powers.

The Rays also condition the color of our auras. Also, the unfolding Lotus and the centers in the planes of personality condition the color of the aura. Naturally the color of the human soul gradually dominates and becomes the undertone of other colors.

As the human soul advances and the Lotus unfolds, you see the aura changing into a rainbow with twelve colors. In ancient writings this rainbow was called "the glory of man."

There is an ancient blessing which says,

> *May your colors never fade away and*
> *may your glory increase year after year.*

Those who are obsessed by destructive thoughts, negative emotions, and harmful actions demonstrate colors that belong to dark forces or to those who serve them. Such colors affect a person psychologically, physically, and even socially. The Tibetan Master describes such colors as "brown, grey, loathsome purple, and lurid greens."

Dark forces or their agents use these colors to cause degeneration in the public consciousness. They even project these colors to cause

- depression, fear, despair, and violence — grey
- carelessness, lust, and corruption — loathsome purple
- hatred, jealousy, slander, and treason — lurid green

It is possible to know the characters of people by knowing the colors they like, the colors by which they decorate their homes, or by the colors of their clothing.

Some artists use the above mentioned colors of dark forces in their art. Some mediums or black magicians use "lurid green and loathsome purple."

Colors form a system of an alphabet of twelve characteristics. A clairvoyant can easily know the character of a man by reading these colors in the aura of the man.

Often the colors appear in front of our eyes at certain times. One can predict the future by noticing the real colors which, in different shapes, pass in front of our eyes.

The creation of the worlds and every kind of true creation follows these steps:

Sound

Color

Form

Sound or tone is related to the mental plane, and those who had an opportunity to dwell in the higher mental plane will be composers and performers of some advanced music.

There are sounds and tones also in the etheric plane which are sources of inspiration for those kinds of music which create crisis, lust, violence, hatred, irresponsibility, separatism, and hypnotic conditions.

The astral or emotional world is the world of color. In the lowest section of the astral plane we have murky, loathsome, grey colors which are the source of irritation and premature stimulation. But when you go higher on the astral plane, the colors become pure, translucent, and irradiating. The higher astral forms have the most amazing color combinations.

The esoteric sound of our thoughts, plans, intentions, and ideas solidify into colors on the corresponding levels of the astral plane. Then they turn into tendencies, habits, actions, and forms.

Most of the time we are the creators of our forms through sound, color, and action.

Chapter 12

Virtues and Healing

Virtues are like the fragrance of flowers. They radiate out as beauty, goodness, and joy, spreading health, energy, and happiness. Each virtue has a different fragrance. A man of virtue is like a bouquet of flowers. Each flower emanates not only its own fragrance but also its own note. On higher planes, a person is perceived as music or as a symphony.

A virtuous person emanates healing powers. Virtues not only heal on the physical plane, but their healing powers also purify space and penetrate to the higher strata of the Subtle Worlds, thus building a channel between the objective and subjective worlds.

The etheric, astral, mental, and higher centers are like flowers which unfold and flourish as the rays of our virtues radiate out from our Inner Core.

Animals smell our emanations. They smell hatred, fear, anger, greed, or jealousy. They also smell joy, love, peace, goodwill, solemnity, and nobility.

A virtuous person radiates his innermost Self, the God within, the Glory within, the creative Source within. The Inner Core is a fiery essence, around which various rings accumulated which limit Its radioactivity. Most of these rings are formed by thoughts, emotions, words, and deeds that are contrary to righteousness, beauty, goodness, purity, light, and love.

Vices are misused virtues. When the polarity of a virtue changes and becomes repulsive, or negative, we develop a vice. You can see this reversal when love changes into hatred, fanaticism, or crime. This is how the Inquisition came into being. In the hearts of His followers, the supreme love of Christ was changed into bitter hatred through the mechanism of dogma, doctrine, and fanaticism. We can still see this going on today in this so-called age of light and freedom. Fanatics in the name of their supreme leader, organize attacks on other religions or faiths which are not blind followers of glamors and illusions, but which exercise compassion, tolerance, and spiritual honesty.

The polarity of a virtue changes because of negative thoughts, emotions, words, and crime. The polarity of the rays changes when the Self identifies with the matter aspect and begins to work for separative interests instead of working for the best interest of all.

Thus, selflessness manifests as consideration for the best interest of all. Selfishness manifests as consideration only for the benefit of a single part. The Self can radiate only when the outer rings change their polarity and allow the rays of the Self to manifest in the form of virtues.

Each manifestation of a virtue is a process of integration, fusion, synthesis, and healing. Any resistance to the outpouring rays of the virtues creates friction. Friction manifests as disease, sickness, or various problems in various levels of the personality.

As the negative walls, or rings, increase around the radiant Nucleus, the person becomes more selfish and more self-destructive. In selfishness the Self identifies Itself with the negative walls of the personality, and the rays of the virtues change into vices.

Vices disintegrate the unity of the organism and its vehicles, and lead the human being to take actions which are against his own survival and progress. In such a state, a person works against himself and becomes his own worst enemy.

On the other side of the picture, a virtuous person is an open magnetic field to the unseen forces of the subjective world, capable of communing with those forces and receiving higher, Cosmic inspirations and impressions. A virtuous person is a focus of benevolent forces. These forces manifest through a virtuous one the way a beam of light shines through a prism. All human progress and all real culture are the result of this communion.

The first sign that one is coming in contact with higher forces is that he manifests beauty in all his relationships. He no longer encourages ugliness, injustice, or vanity but stands for beauty, for principles.

The first time a person establishes contact with higher principles, he develops a system of censorship within his personality. From that moment on, he clearly observes all his actions and eliminates those actions which do not agree with higher principles. This censorship is the manifestation of the conscience. He now has a conscience and is on his way to becoming a true human being. Censorship eventually turns into an inner command post, which gradually eliminates all opposition to light, righteousness, beauty, joy, serenity, solemnity, and so on. As the personality is tuned in with higher principles and with the rays of the Self, it manifests health, happiness, joy, and energy.

Virtues

- striving
- courage
- daring
- discrimination
- solemnity
- harmlessness
- service
- compassion
- patience
- fearlessness

— gratitude
— responsibility
— enthusiasm
— sacrifice
— nobility

Each virtue is related to one of the parts of the body. Each virtue has its own color, its own fragrance, its own note, its own motion, and its own octaves. On each octave, it manifests differently and forms major or minor keys. Octaves are divided into higher and lower octaves. In higher octaves, the virtue is closer to its archetype and channels tremendous energy. When integration is achieved, lower octaves are used to manifest the charge of higher octaves.

Each virtue is a ray from one of the zodiacal signs. This ray passes through one of the petals of the twelve-petaled Lotus, or Chalice, and turns into a virtue. Every virtue is a power with a very strong charge, unless it is distorted or broken by glamors, illusions, and maya existing in the body. Each virtue eventually creates a salt in the aura, and then in the physical body, which keeps the body healthy and in tune with the Zodiac.

The first twelve virtues mentioned above are related to our Zodiac. The last three are related to the Greater Zodiac:

• Enthusiasm is related to the Great Bear
• Sacrifice is related to Sirius
• Nobility is related to Orion

The following is a table of the twelve virtues, their related zodiacal sign, and the mineral salts which they form in our body:

Virtues - Zodiacal Signs - Salts

Virtue	Zodiacal Sign	Mineral Salts
Striving	Aries	potassium phosphate (kali phosphate)
Courage	Leo	magnesium phosphoricum
Daring	Capricorn	calcium phosphate
Harmlessness	Gemini	kali muriaticum
Solemnity	Virgo	kali sulfuricum
Service	Pisces	ferrum phosphate
Discrimination	Cancer	calcareum fluoricum
Responsibility	Libra	natrum phosphate
Gratitude	Taurus	natrum sulphuretum
Fearlessness	Scorpio	calcium sulfate
Patience	Sagittarius	silica
Compassion	Aquarius	natrum muriaticum

Each zodiacal sign emanates a certain energy which builds these salts in the body via the etheric body. For example, Aries is *potassium phosphate* (*kali phosphate*). It is activated in our body and assimilated from the emanations of Aries when a person demonstrates the virtue of striving. Unless the virtue of striving is active, a person cannot assimilate *potassium phosphate* from Aries. Aries rules the cerebrum. We are told that *kali phosphate* unites albumen with oxygen and produces the grey matter of the brain.

Striving increases *kali phosphate* and eliminates many troubles from the body, such as depression, nervous disorders, insomnia, irritation, and certain kinds of insanity. Striving is a great virtue of the human soul. In exercising striving, a person cures himself of many diseases.

Courage is a virtue which produces *magnesium phosphoricum*. This is a very important salt which forms especially when the Sun is in Leo. This salt is transmitted through the Sun to our etheric body, where the emanation of Leo is registered and changed into *magnesium phosphoricum* via the fire of courage. Every act of courage increases this salt in our body. Courage heals headaches, menstrual problems, colic, heart trouble, and tension. In every act of courage we see a tremendous increase in the presence of *phosphoricum* in the body.

Daring is related to Capricorn and creates *calcium phosphate* when the Sun is in the sign of Capricorn. But without the virtue of daring, the rays of the sign impress our etheric body or aura but do not produce *calcium phosphate*.

It is true that *calcium phosphate* can be taken from outside sources, but it cannot be assimilated by the body unless the fire of daring is kindled in the aura. Lack of *calcium phosphate* causes tooth decay, skin diseases, anemia, curvature of the spine, and many other problems.

Daring puts the digestive fluids into action. Every time you have indigestion, it is because you have given up something beautiful and constructive; you have given up your daring. Daring people can eat and digest almost anything.

Harmlessness is the virtue of Gemini. The rays of Gemini change into *kali muriaticum* when the fire of harmlessness is present in the aura. This salt is important for catarrh, swollen glands, sore throats, swollen tonsils, chicken pox, and enlarged rheumatic joints. Those who are harmless can easily manufacture *kali muriaticum* and eliminate the above-mentioned troubles. Harmfulness saps the reservoir of this salt and opens a person to the attacks of various diseases.

Solemnity is a virtue which produces *kali sulfuricum* in the aura, especially when the Sun is in Virgo. This element is essential. Lack of it creates dandruff, gastroduodenal catarrh, anemia, and bronchitis. By increasing the virtue of solemnity in our life, we produce this precious substance in our body, which lubricates and purifies the whole body mechanism.

Service is the name of an energy which makes a person radioactive. This energy evokes the soul or spiritual aspect in people and helps them proceed on the path toward liberation and perfection. When the Sun is in Pisces, the energy or spirit of service creates *ferrum* *phosphate*. This salt is very important for the body. Lack of it causes various inflammations, congestions, headaches, insomnia, lumbago, emotional disturbances, weak heart, bruises, depression, and apathy. Service eliminates all such troubles by producing *ferrum phosphate*.

Discrimination is the seventh virtue. When the Sun is in Cancer, discrimination produces *calcareum fluoricum*. This is a precious salt needed by the body. Its lack creates trouble in the bones, teeth, and muscles and forms splits between the toes or fingers, at the anus, behind the ears, and so on. When the virtue of discrimination is exercised daily in our thoughts, words, and actions, *calcareum fluoricum* builds up and heals or prevents the various troubles mentioned above.

Responsibility is a virtue which creates *natrum phosphate*, especially at the time when our Sun is in Libra. Lack of this salt creates kidney troubles, rheumatic troubles, gout, worms, diabetes, bladder disorders, and gallstones. In raising the sense of responsibility, one can cure himself from the above-mentioned diseases because the fire of responsibility creates *natrum phosphate* in your aura, which passes into your body and works miracles.

Gratitude is the virtue of Taurus. When the Sun is in Taurus, the fire of gratitude creates *natrum sulphuretum*. This salt protects you from malaria, biliousness, chills, and fever; it eliminates excessive water from your system and cures vascular spasms. This salt is created through gratitude. The spirit of gratitude can eliminate many physical and emotional troubles, helping you feel content and happy.

Gratitude heals thyroid troubles and helps the thyroid purify many toxins in the body. Ungrateful people accumulate toxins in their thyroid. They hurt their heart and tense the solar plexus, which reacts upon the digestive tract.

Fearlessness is a great virtue which creates *calcium sulfate* when the Sun is in Scorpio. A lack of this salt produces stomach troubles, ulcers, boils, carbuncles, kidney, and pancreatic troubles.

Fearlessness cures the body of many diseases by producing *calcium sulfate* in the aura and in the body. Those who are fearful eventually lose all deposits of this important salt.

Patience produces *silica*, especially at the time when the Sun is in Sagittarius. A lack of *silica* causes complications in the perspiration system, the eyelids, bones, tonsils, throat, ears, hair, and nails. As one increases in this virtue, he cures himself of many physical troubles and emotional and mental tensions. Impatience saps the deposits of *silica* and makes a person subject to various attacks. Patience also stabilizes the higher mind and helps us to think on abstract levels.

Patience regulates the urinary and digestive systems. The bowels work better as a person exercises more patience. The glandular system functions more harmoniously and produces those elements necessary for health. Patience strengthens the generative organs and invigorates the whole nervous system. A hurried life is the cause of many diseases.

Compassion is the twelfth virtue, the fire of which creates *natrum muriaticum*, especially when the Sun is in Aquarius. In developing compassion we increase our health and live a long, healthy, peaceful life.

Lack of compassion in the form of cruelty, hatred, or crime saps the deposits of *natrum muriaticum* and leads to colds, constipation, shingles, blisters, eczema, sunstroke, malaria, indigestion, hay fever, and irritation. Compassion cures all of these.

Compassion also purifies the blood. Those who need to purify their blood must exercise compassion. It also activates the liver, which then expels the toxins which have accumulated in it.

Compassion vitalizes the etheric body and makes it more receptive to the vital currents in space. It is possible to transform the whole personality through compassion.

In the future, physicians will analyze a person from the standpoint of his virtues and prescribe virtues for him. A doctor will say, for example, "If you want to eliminate your cold, enlarged tonsils, or swollen glands, you must start exercising striving, daring, and harmlessness." This will be the beginning of the biochemistry of the virtues. More virtues will be analyzed and related to various parts of the organs, and the organs will be cured through virtues, or scientifically-guided spiritual living.

Each virtue is also related to a note, to a sound. It is possible to create certain salts in the human aura through playing certain music in which a certain note predominates.

It is also important to know the relationship between zodiacal signs and their rulers. There are esoteric and exoteric rulers. Esoteric rulers are active when a man is an accepted disciple. Exoteric rulers are for average humanity. In *Esoteric Astrology*,[1] the rulers of the zodiacal signs are given as follows:

Zodiacal Signs and Rulers

Sign	Exoteric Ruler	Esoteric Ruler	Hierarchical Ruler
Aries	Mars	Mercury	Uranus
Taurus	Venus	Vulcan	Vulcan
Gemini	Mercury	Venus	Earth
Cancer	Moon	Neptune	Neptune
Leo	Sun	Sun	Sun
Virgo	Mercury	Moon (veiling a planet)	Jupiter
Libra	Venus	Uranus	Saturn
Scorpio	Mars	Mars	Mercury
Sagittarius	Jupiter	Earth	Mars
Capricorn	Saturn	Saturn	Venus
Aquarius	Uranus	Jupiter	Moon
Pisces	Jupiter	Pluto	Pluto

1. Alice A. Bailey, *Esoteric Astrology*, pp. 68, 86.

This information can be used in several ways. One can find the virtue/salt of a given sign and then tie in that sign's esoteric and exoteric rulers to discover what parts of the body are affected. For example, let us take Aries.

If the virtue of striving is exercised in Aries, *potassium phosphate (kali phosphate)* is created. Aries is related to the cerebrum. The exoteric ruler of Aries is Mars; the esoteric ruler is Mercury. Mars is related to the left cerebrum; Mercury is related to the thyroid. A deficiency of *potassium phosphate* will affect the left cerebrum if the man is average, but it will affect the thyroid if he is on the path of discipleship. Striving will eliminate both troubles because it will generate the needed salt. If, together with striving, the note, color, and movement of the virtue are used at the time when the Sun is in Aries, recovery from the illness will proceed very rapidly.

Man is part of the whole system of Nature. He must have an occasional tune-up so that he synchronizes with the energies of the Cosmos. The secret of health is the secret of synchronization with the forces of Nature.

Let us look at this process and how it relates to virtues by taking the example of the first virtue, striving.

Striving starts from within. It is the presence by which the Inner Core tries to master Its vehicles and life. In striving, you make efforts to surpass yourself. No matter in what you are engaged, you try to do it better and better in the light of beauty, goodness, and truth. You try to work better in your home, your office, school, and so on. You try to surpass your former level of knowledge, awareness, and beingness.

As you can see, striving has many octaves. There are physical octaves, emotional octaves, and mental octaves. In lower octaves you must improve your behavior, your way of walking, talking, moving, gesturing, your relationships with others. Then on higher octaves, you must improve your emotions and emotional relationships. On still higher octaves, you must improve your mental activities, thoughts, and mental relationships. On still higher octaves, you must deepen your Intuition, and so on.

There are seven octaves; each virtue can be exercised on all seven planes of your being. The physical, emotional, and mental planes are the exoteric field; the higher planes are the esoteric field.

Striving increases only when you have opposition, difficulties, obstacles, and hindrances. Luxury and an easy life kill the spirit of striving and deprive you of those salts necessary for the health of your body. Striving produces a tonic for the brain, nervous system, and spleen. These are the main network through which prana is received and used. When the Great Ones emphasize virtue, They are really telling us that virtue means health.

Those who are criminal, insane, or barbaric are unhealthy people who lack virtue. Their lives have no balance or equilibrium.

As another example, the next virtue, courage exercised in Leo, produces *magnesium phosphoricum*. This is a salt which keeps the balance between the acids and the normal fluids of the body. Through courage one can overcome troubles related to the kidneys, pancreas, bladder, some skin diseases, and gallstones.

The exoteric and esoteric rulers of Leo are the Sun. The Sun is related to the spleen, solar plexus, and heart. Disorders related to the spleen and solar plexus can be healed through exercising and developing courage, especially when the Sun is in Leo. Through courage one strengthens his heart and eliminates many kinds of heart problems. In accepted discipleship, when courage is lacking, heart troubles begin to appear. An accepted disciple must always exercise courage upon many octaves.

Courage is the power to detach yourself from your not-self and identify yourself with your Real Self. The moment you identify with your Real Self, you feel the energy and power to overcome hindrances and obstacles on the path of the expanding light, love, and freedom of your True Self.

Virtues accumulate psychic energy within the network of your etheric body and in your Chalice. It is this energy which produces all the chemicals you need, all the salts necessary to cure your body and sustain your health for a long time.

Psychic energy is the elixir of life, the essence of all virtues, which not only revitalizes your threefold nature but also puts you in contact with Cosmic sources of light and harmony.

Chapter 13

Sound and the Aura

The aura is very sensitive to color and sound, but sound contains color and is far superior to color. Right sound purifies the aura. It energizes, vitalizes, and harmonizes the aura, resulting in good health.

If a person tells lies, curses, uses blasphemy or dirty talk, he pollutes his aura. Silence makes the aura recharge itself. High-level speech energizes the aura.

In the near future, great doctors will heal sicknesses by giving their patients certain notes to sound. Future healers will be highly clairvoyant, able to see which part of the aura is fading and which part is congested or over-stimulated. They will give their patients certain notes to sound in combination with certain rhythms and durations, and by doing so clean any problem from its roots. Many sicknesses originate in the astral and mental auras, and by removing the roots of disease, one can enjoy perfect health.

Depression is jellification of the aura. When the aura becomes dense and jellylike, you feel inertia and depression. Depressed people attract into their auras dark forces, who hate harmonious clear tones. The best way to come out of depression is to sound the scale after breathing deeply. Sounding helps to "de-gel" the aura and restore your joy and enthusiasm for life.

Sound rearranges the atoms of our aura and our bones. It has a very potent effect on our glamors, illusions, and maya. If scientifically used, it may be the answer to most of our needs.

For a start, it is necessary to learn how to sound the musical scale up and down, with four vowels. The four vowels are:

- a pronounced as "ah"
- o pronounced as "oh"
- u pronounced as "oo" (as in ooze)
- e pronounced as "ee" (as in feet)

Sit or stand in a comfortable position and, beginning with C, sing the scale for five minutes daily:

- c, d, e, f, g, a, b, c — on "ah"
- c, d, e, f, g, a, b, c — on "oh"
- c, d, e, f, g, a, b, c — on "oo"
- c, d, e, f, g, a, b, c — on "ee"

At the beginning of each scale, groan or sigh. Then take a deep breath and sound the vowels. When going up

the scale, close the right eye. When going down, close
the left eye. After doing this for fifteen days, you will
then be ready to perform this exercise using seven vowels:

"eh"	as in set
"ah"	as in art
"e"	as in feet
"ieu"	as in adieu
"oo"	as in ooze
"uh"	as in hurt
"oh"	as in oak

For the first ten days, breathe in between each note.
Then for the next twenty days, sound the whole scale
(seven notes) in one breath.

The intoning of each sound will be more effective
if you remember the colors of the notes and vowels. You
can use the following colors for each note:

Notes and Colors

Note	*Color*
C	red
D	orange
E	yellow
F	yellow-green
G	blue-green
A	blue-violet
B	red-violet

If you want to make this exercise even more effective, you can focus your mind on the following thoughts for each note:

Notes - Colors - Virtues

Note	Color	Virtue
C	red	striving
D	orange	harmlessness
E	yellow	courage
F	yellow-green	solemnity
G	blue-green	fearlessness
A	blue-violet	daring
B	red-violet	service

You do not need to direct your sound to any part of your body. Your entire body, emotional, and mental vehicles act as a sounding board. Very soon you will feel how your voice creates special vibrations in your vehicles.

This is one of the best ways to purify and energize your body, and to destroy accumulations of glamor, illusion, and maya. When you sound the seven vowels with the right facial movements, tonality, and purity, you charge the seven head centers and their correspondences in the three lower vehicles. Sounding the seven vowels will cleanse and purify many obstacles within the aura, if the exercise is carried out with one-pointed concentration.

As the human aura develops and a greater amount of fusion is achieved between the auras of human beings and between the human and devic kingdoms, the illusion of privacy will gradually vanish not only in mental realms but also in our daily lives and in all our relationships.

The evolution of humanity shows that in the future, ownership of any kind will be obsolete. Starting with houses, land, tools, and means of transportation, individual ownership will defer to group ownership, group ownership to national ownership, and national ownership to international ownership. The economy, communication systems, and computers will make individual ownership an impossibility. Privacy will vanish; a person's life will be common knowledge to anyone who wants to know about it. Your bank account, travel plans, business transactions, failures, and successes — even your individual relationships — will lose their privacy and become part of common knowledge.

The time will come in which people will be able to see your motives, your thoughts, and the direction of your thoughts. All of this will be possible because the Self scattered in every form is collecting Itself and beginning to act as the One Self. As the One Self occupies more territory and the number of people who are aware of the One Self increases, more people will live in the consciousness of a unified Self. Such progress will produce its outer tools, such as computers, x-rays, laser beams, solar energy, and so on, which will work in many forms to annihilate separatism, upon which most of that which we call privacy or private interest is built.

History shows this very clearly. Five hundred years ago, a person had his own castle, his own street, his own money, his own personal secrets (which he could keep), and his own horse. Today, we have our condominiums, apartments, colleges, universities, computers, trains, airplanes, banks, libraries — and seventy percent of our ownership has become public ownership.

Five hundred years ago you were practically stuck to your house, to your town, to your race. At present, a person can live in any hotel in the world, travel almost anywhere via any kind of transportation he chooses, and find the accommodations he wants or needs. He can marry or have a relationship with people from every nationality or race.

In the past you were the slave of your faith, philosophy, or tradition. Now all religions, philosophies, and traditions are open to you. Of course, there are still separating walls. These structures that have been built in the past centuries cannot be taken down all at once, in just one minute, or in one hundred years. The currents must be directed into the right channels.

Synthesis takes time, but it needs human cooperation to alleviate the pain and suffering caused by separatism. Historical events will eventually prove that there is only the One Self in all humanity. All individuals are cells. Nations and races are organs and systems in one body. And the time will come when all these separate units will consciously function in relation to the One Self.

Such a realization will be the greatest breakthrough of the consciousness of the race. It will alleviate all waste, pollution, animosity, competition, pain, and suffering from the earth. The new race will be composed of those who contain the seeds of these concepts within themselves. Those who pass away informed about these ideas and concepts will bloom and flourish in the Subtle Worlds, and when they come back into incarnation, they will be like lions on the path of evolution. Such an evolution is not only possible, but it is a Cosmic law from which no one can escape. Escape is possible only for a short time, resulting in a heavy cost of pain and suffering. In the long run, the law will impose itself in order to bring about total synthesis.

In the higher centers of learning in the subjective dimensions, the emphasis and goal of all learning and planning, in all branches of knowledge at this time, is synthesis. Those who pass away with these concepts and ideas, with a realization of the One Self and synthesis, will be readily admitted into the colleges and universities of the supermundane world in preparation to become candidates for the next super-race.

In the past, success was measured by the power of separate interests. In the future, success will be measured by the intensity of your ability to synthesize. Success will be measured not by the power to have, separate, and use but by the power to give, unite, and be useful.

In the years to come, people will see the futility of privacy and individual ownership. The conductor of the symphony is the Self, and the Self will annihilate every kind of friction and hide-and-seek between each and all of Its members. All will come under the light of synthesis, whose symbol is a radiant aura.

How the Aura is Hurt

Abrupt movements hurt the aura. Initiates do not perform sudden movements. They have a certain rhythm in walking or moving their hands and body. Rhythmic movement strengthens the aura. Dancing, hard work, and body movements are considered beneficial if they incorporate certain rhythms.

The aura is very sensitive to the energy radiating out of the eyes. The aura can feel a glance. It is known that a well-intentioned glance can bring blessings into the aura, while glances charged with ugly motives disturb the aura immensely.

The glance of an advanced Initiate can bring a great amount of blessing to a crowd, while the glance of an evil person disturbs the whole aura. This is why advanced Ashrams are restricted to those whose hearts and motives are full of goodness and beauty.

If a person gives you a dirty look, the force coming from his eyes can disturb or even damage your aura. Very soon the radiation of the eyes will be measured. It is interesting to note that any disturbance in the aura affects the eyes first; the eyes are very closely connected to the aura. When the aura of a pregnant woman is damaged, the eyes of her child will be weak and will require permanent attention.

Temporary disturbances in the aura have long-range effects on the eyes. When the aura is in harmony, the eyesight improves considerably. Our own eyes can even weaken when we receive visitors whose auras are in bad shape.

In the presence of a spiritually-advanced person, our eyesight improves. Communication with advanced disciples and great Teachers considerably improves our eyesight because their rhythmic auras bring peace and harmony into our aura.

When the higher bodies begin to let their radiation flow into the aura, one can see ruby-colored sparks around the periphery of the aura. Purple and blue auras belong to advanced disciples.

Singing or sounding the musical scale or even talking radiates electromagnetic energies into the aura. All day long we think, visualize, imagine, and wish and thus accumulate many mental, emotional, and etheric formations within our aura. Every time we hate or are afraid of something, we identify ourselves with that object; we build in our aura an image or form of that which we are afraid of or hate.

Every time we imagine, visualize, or talk about a problem or person, we build certain forms of the problem or person in our aura. Each mental, emotional, and physical reaction or response creates a specific form within the aura. We may add to these the forms that are projected upon our aura by other people through their thoughts, imagination, and speech. Thus, we see how many forms and patterns fill our aura daily.

Sometimes the aura is so polluted by such accumulations and contradictory currents that we live in the contaminated pool of our subtle forms. Fortunately, Nature has ways to partially clear this pool. For example, lofty thoughts, pure and loving emotions, and singing or lecturing on high-level subjects purify the aura and make it ready to go another round.

The best way to purify the aura and make it healthy and beautiful is to use three formulas given to us in the Ageless Wisdom:

    1. develop lofty thoughts

    2. develop high aspirations

    3. sound these ideas and aspirations through the musical scale, starting with middle C, or sing your ideas with deep aspiration and joy

Daily efforts in these directions can purify the aura because pure thought, lofty emotion, and singing destroy crystallizations in our aura and create harmony and purity.

Nature always provides the keys to our problems if we are alert. People use their voices to handle many problems. For example, we sigh, or we make different kinds of sounds when we are

- afraid
- disappointed
- in pain

• joyful
• excited
• surprised

These sighs or sounds create certain favorable conditions in our aura which help us handle conditions more creatively. We can use our voice or sing in order to

• release ourselves from pain, or to alleviate pain
• avoid a painful experience
• overcome depression
• deeply enjoy a pleasure or sensation

The overall accumulation of sound impressions determine the condition of our aura. Every formation in our aura has an effect on our mind, emotions, and body, and upon our thinking, feeling, and health.

These crystallized formations must not stay within our aura too long if we want to have a healthy aura in which energies flow unblocked by subtle forms or crystallizations.

We must do our meditation daily and create lofty thoughts or victorious thoughts. These thoughts can destroy and purify our aura from any mental crystallizations and greatly contribute to mental health.

Contact with beauty in Nature, painting, music, writing, dancing, and other fields of the arts creates pure aspiration in our heart and helps us purify our aura from coarse desires, wishes, and identifications.

Inspiration comes to us from higher sources of creative energy or higher beings. Impressions are the creative sources of our thoughts. All these come to the aura and are received in their pure condition, are distorted, or rejected. If the aura is prepared for reception, it becomes a creative mechanism through which greater beauty is manifested to the world. Good deeds, labor, and sacrificial acts clear the etheric aura in particular and the whole aura in general.

Above all, sound has a great influence upon our whole aura. For example, sound used for lying, cursing, blasphemy, or malice creates acidic conditions in the aura, which damage and weaken certain parts of the aura. Ill will is a destructive form in the aura; harmful thoughts, thoughts charged with hatred, animosity, and destruction blacken the aura.

It is very beneficial for the aura if we speak about our lofty thoughts and about our highest aspirations and directions oriented toward the welfare of humanity. The voice carries a purifying, constructive, and harmonizing influence into the aura if it comes from a pure heart or from an enlightened mind.

In the Teaching, we are told that we must not imitate animals. By doing so, we create heavy disturbances in our aura or impress it with the form of the animal we imitate. The animal form, being associated with our past, can stimulate whatever has been left in our aura from the past and pull us back toward retrogression. There is also the danger of inviting or attracting an animal spirit into your aura by creating a "voice tunnel" for its descent.

The sound created by wind through the trees is very beneficial and has a healing effect on your mental aura.

The sounds of waterfalls and flowing rivers and streams are extremely beneficial to the astral aura, if the right distance from them is found.

The songs of birds are extremely invigorating for the etheric and physical aura. They not only transmit certain energies into the aura, but they also purify it from many crystallizations. In certain esoteric schools, singing birds were kept near the temples so that their melodies could be heard day and night.

The sound of thunder is very beneficial; it clears away many ugly formations in space and in our aura. In certain esoteric schools, thunder was met with great exaltation and joy.

Mechanical noise from cars, airplanes, factories, and various equipment is very harmful to the aura, especially to the glands and nervous system. The electronic waves to which humanity is subjected day and night are one of the main reasons why people cannot make a breakthrough into higher psychic realms. Sounds emanated from these waves petrify those threads of psychic development which put us in contact with higher worlds.

Only very gifted persons with highly developed auras can transcend the barriers created by electronic waves, which have almost sealed the space around the world. Contemporary science will one day realize how its discoveries have prepared a dungeon for the human soul.

Electronic musical instruments, loudspeakers, and the amplification of certain instruments carry a high voltage of a destructive element which is harmful to the auras of humans, animals and plants. In the future, the destructive effects they have created in the auras of living forms will be discovered. Telephone conversations also have a very heavy effect on the aura around the head and ears.

We must also remember that each element has its specific note. It will be possible in the future to move an object or create changes in it just by transmitting the conditioning thought energy via a specific note. Sound is always absorbed and transmitted to any object, form, or living entity through its aura.

Nature communicates not through form, but through the aura of the form. Later it will become possible to teach how to nullify the effect of electronic waves through certain invocations, songs, and music in order to penetrate into higher realms.

It is very beneficial to carry on your daily conversations using the keynote of your sun sign, and to deliver a message or lecture in the keynote of your rising sign.

Music created by advanced Initiates can be extremely helpful for the purification and development of the aura. If such music is found, it must be listened to not only with the ear but with the entire aura.

Music created by those who have no interest in the spiritual development of humanity can greatly damage the aura. For example, disco music, acid rock, and the like distort the aura and prepare the destruction of the spiritual man.

Music which uses woodwind instruments is more effective than the music of any other instrument. The human voice, however, is the most effective sound in the world.

Each part of the body and each organ has a specific note. The various notes in Nature feed them. Each body or vehicle is built by chords; if we find these chords or keynotes, we are better able to heal our body or organs by sounding these notes and transmitting the sound to the organ through the aura.

We not only have keynotes for our vehicles but also for each of our organs or body parts. The ancients knew this science, but because of its misuse it was withdrawn approximately fifty thousand years ago.

Man will gradually realize that he is built by his own voice. In the future, esoteric schools will teach these principles, once humanity has overcome its separatism, fanaticism, religious and traditional vanities, and approaches life with a pure heart and with sincere dedication to the service of humanity.

When our aura unfolds and refines itself, it becomes possible to receive greater assistance from the Subtle Worlds. The inhabitants of the Subtle Worlds, being aware of the conditions, pain, suffering, and vanity in the world, try to warn, guide, and lead us toward a better life which is acceptable to the Subtle Worlds. Such guidance and help is given to us in the Subtle Worlds, where we penetrate every time we sleep. Such guidance often takes the form of a dream or vision, which can easily fade away without impression.

To receive clear guidance, one must develop his heart, purify it, and increase in it the fire of Spirit. The element of fire must be found in the heart and aura if one wants to communicate with the Subtle Worlds. Fire is the active presence of Spirit. This fire does not usually exist within the aura, vehicles, and heart except when they are permeated by that fire because of a life lived according to the principles of

- Beauty
- Goodness
- Righteousness
- Joy
- Freedom
- Harmlessness
- Enthusiasm

If the man violates these principles, he extinguishes the fire in his aura and heart. If he lives within these principles, the fire extends and permeates all parts of his aura and heart, and builds a bridge between the Subtle Worlds. Nothing can be achieved without this fire.

As the fire of the Spirit purifies the aura and permeates all parts of the human being and organism, it attracts higher fires from higher beings, until the fire of the Cosmic Heart blends with the fire of Spirit. It is through linking with the higher fires that conscious contact with higher worlds or planes is achieved.

Fire is very important, but of equal importance is purity of heart. Fire focuses itself only within the heart; from the heart, it permeates throughout the aura and body. If the heart is not pure, the accumulating fire can burn the petals of the heart, bringing great disaster to the vehicles of the person. It must also be added that contact with the Subtle Worlds is registered only in the heart, on the screen of the focused fire.

The unfolding heart center orchestrates all the movements and colors of the aura, and imports into it those impressions received from the Subtle Worlds. Thus, each vehicle — mental, astral, etheric, and physical — is informed of the contact through various impressions.

There are currents of thought, emotion, and action that hurt the heart center and cause great damage in the aura. One of these is irritation. Irritation appears in the aura as red and black dots, or like red and black balls which pulsate and move in parallel lines like worms. They sometimes stretch themselves and fuse with each other, forming horizontal lines of black and red mixed together. This is the condition which precipitates imperil into the nadis and upon the nerve channels. After this occurs, irritation in the aura becomes very contagious.

We are told that irritation is weakness of will. Every time we lose control over our aura, irritation takes over. Will energy is dynamic energy which protects the aura from various fluctuations. It is steady radiance which repels disturbing influences coming from either outside or inside.

Will is the power which sustains the flow of energies in the aura and keeps the colors shining, in harmony and stability. Every time will power weakens, outer and inner influences distort the equilibrium and bring in various disturbances.

Irritation is the result of negative thoughts, emotions, and attitudes. Will energy, being the highest fire of the human being, does not tolerate such formations within the aura. It also repels similar waves coming from outside the man.[1]

Actually, irritation is not the only culprit. All moral weaknesses, habits, hang-ups, and vices are the result of weaknesses of will. Any time the will weakens, maya, glamor, illusion, and inner and outer distortions attack the aura. The solution to many weaknesses lies in education of course, but primarily it lies in the strengthening of the will.

It has been predicted that an "aura meter" will be invented in the future, that will electromagnetically read the condition of the aura on a very sensitive screen. The colors of the aura will be translated as sounds, fluctuations, movements, or noise. A completely new alphabet will be created to translate the condition of the aura from color to sound. The impressions received from the aura will be categorized, and the conditions of the higher spheres of the aura will be known. Thus, the keynotes of the bodies will be found.

The healing of the bodies will proceed through sounds and the harmonization of the notes of their aura and their rhythm. One can imagine a huge building

---

1. For further information, read *Irritation, The Destructive Fire.*

Constellations - Virtues - Rays - Colors - Notes

Constellation

Planets*	Virtue	Ray	Color	Note
Aries 6, 4, 7	Striving	7	Red	C
Taurus 5, 1, 1	Gratitude	4	Red-orange	C#
Gemini 4, 5, 3	Harmlessness	2, 3	Orange	D
Cancer 4, 6, 6	Discrimination	7	Yellow-orange	D#
Leo 2, 2, 2	Courage	1, 5	Yellow	E
Virgo 4, 4, 2	Solemnity	2, 6	Yellow-green	F
Libra 5, 7, 3	Responsibility	3	Green	F#
Scorpio 6, 6, 4	Fearlessness	4	Blue-green	G
Sagittarius 2, 3, 6	Patience	4,5,6	Blue	G#
Capricorn 3, 3, 5	Daring	1,3,7	Blue-violet	A
Aquarius 7, 2, 4	Compassion	5	Violet	A#
Pisces 2, 1, 1	Service	2, 6	Red-violet	B

*= Exoteric, Esoteric, Hierarchical Rays of Ruling Planets

equipped with aura meters and harmonizers, or doctors who teach the esoteric science of sounding the right note with the right visualization and movements to heal people from various psychological disturbances and ailments.

Zodiacal Signs - Rulers/Rays

Sign	Exoteric Ruler/Ray	Esoteric Ruler/Ray	Hierarchial Ruler/Ray
1. Aries	Mars/6	Mercury/4	Uranus/7
2. Taurus	Venus/5	Vulcan/1	Vulcan/1
3. Gemini	Mercury/4	Venus/5	Earth/3
4. Cancer	Moon/4	Neptune/6	Neptune/6
5. Leo	Sun/2	Sun/2	Sun/2
6. Virgo	Mercury/4	Moon/4	Jupiter/2
7. Libra	Venus/5	Uranus/7	Saturn/3
8. Scorpio	Mars/6	Mars/6	Mercury/4
9. Sagittarius	Jupiter/2	Saturn/3	Mars/6
10. Capricorn	Saturn/3	Saturn/3	Venus/5
11. Aquarius	Uranus/7	Jupiter/2	Moon/4
12. Pisces	Jupiter/2	Pluto/1	Pluto/1

Numbers - Planets - Rays

Number	Planet	Ray
1	Vulcan	1
2	Pluto	1
3	Mercury	4

4	Moon	4 (substitute)
5	Venus	5
6	Jupiter	2
7	Sun	2 (substitute)
8	Saturn	3
9	Earth	3
10	Neptune	6
11	Mars	6
12	Uranus	7

Notes and Rays of Constellations

Constellation	Notes	Rays	Combination
Aries	C	1	
Taurus	C#	4	
Gemini	D	2	
Cancer	D#		3-7
Leo	E		1-5
Virgo	F		2-6
Libra	F#	3	
Scorpio	G	4	
Sagittarius	G#		4,5,6
Capricorn	A		1,3,7
Aquarius	A#	5	
Pisces	B		2-6

Playing the wrong music for the wrong person saps his salts. Wrong colors create sickness. When this relationship is scientifically investigated, we will not need hospitals — only temples of wisdom where people can go to increase their virtues through proper music, sound, and energy.

Energy is the radiation of great constellations which can be properly channeled through special colors, special sounds, and virtues. Thus, health is a spiritual matter; the cure of disease depends upon the virtues of the soul.[2]

We are told some interesting points regarding keynotes and constellations:

1. The keynote of Aries is C major, which has no sharps or flats.

2. The keynote of Taurus is C# major, which has seven sharps: F#, C# ,G#, D#, A#, E#, and B#.

3. The keynote of Gemini is D major, which has two sharps: F# and C#.

4. The keynote of Cancer is D# major, which has five sharps and two double sharps: F##, C##, G#, D#, A#, E#, B#.

5. The keynote of Leo is E major, which has four sharps: F#, C#, G#, D#.

---

2. For further information, read *New Dimensions in Healing*.

6. The keynote of Virgo is F major, which has one flat: B flat

7. The keynote of Libra is F# major, which has six sharps: F#, C#, G#, D#, A#, E#.

8. The keynote of Scorpio is G major, which has one sharp: F#.

9. The keynote of Sagittarius is G# major, which has six sharps and one double sharp: F##, C#, G#, D#, A#, E#, B#.

10. The keynote of Capricorn is A major, which has three sharps: F#, C#, G#.

11. The keynote of Aquarius is A# major, which has four sharps and three double sharps: F##, C##, G##, D#, A#, E#, B#.

12. The keynote of Pisces is B major, which has five sharps: F#, C#, G#, D#, A#.

Thus, when the virtues are combined with the right music and colors, certain salts come into being.

Each zodiacal sign also has its own type of movement which creates a release of a certain energy, certain colors, and certain fragrances.

Vibrations of Sound

In the chromatic scale we have twelve notes: C, C#, D, D#, E, F, F#, G, G#, A, A#, B.

Middle C vibrates at 256 cycles per second. It is audible at not more than 9 times 256. For example, if we multiply 256 by 9, we have 2,304 vibrations per second.

If the astral ear is open, it will hear this level of C. This C manifests in the astral plane as the color red.

In the mental plane we see arrow-like forms in red when the vibration rises to 20,736. In the Intuitional Plane, C produces fire. We call it solar fire. Solar fire starts from the higher mind and goes to the lower Intuitional Plane. (The three higher levels of the mental plane form the Intuitional Plane.) This solar fire is registered when C rises to 186,624 vibrations per second. Solar fire manifests as light.

On the Atmic Plane, C is registered as electric fire when it reaches 1,679,616 vibrations per second. This is pure love. On the Monadic Plane, C expresses itself as purest Divine Will. It is interesting to note that the highest vibration of any element fuses with Divine Will. When we add the numbers representing the vibrations per second, we have the following comparisons:

- 256=4 (2+5+6=13; 3+1=4). 4 is the symbol of the lower square.
- 2,304=9; 9 is the number of the astral plane. This is a great mystery. The astral plane is directly connected to the Monad, and is the reflection of the Intuitional Plane.
- 20,736=9 on the Mental Plane.
- 186,624=9 on the Intuitional Plane.
- 1,679,616=9 on the Atmic Plane.
- 136,048,896=9 on the Divine Plane.

Curiously enough, if we add the numbers of all seven planes, we get 4.

$$4+9+9+9+9+9+9 = 58; \; 5+8 = 13 \; ; \; 1+3 = 4$$

The number nine equals the C major note, which is red.

When we sound OM with a pure, clear C note and raise its vibration emotionally, mentally, intuitively, atmically, monadically, and divinely, we will be able to use its vibration on all of these planes, bringing corresponding movement and changes in them, while in the meantime coordinating the actions of all planes.

Each plane corresponds to a center on the planet. This center is contacted through sounding its note. Each center has seven spirilla, and each note evokes the corresponding spirilla of the center.

Sharp notes are catalystic sounds in the same planes.

Red – C

Red C is related to prostatic ganglia, mesenteric plexus and the adrenals. It is also related to the etheric "base of spine" center where the fire of kundalini rests. The generative organs are influenced by red and also by the note C. Iron has a great affinity for the color red and the note C. We must remember that elements are found on all planes. For example, we have physical iron, astral, mental, and intuitional iron, and so on.

Red and the note C are related to the First Ray of Power, which is the source of energy, strength, courage, daring, and forward-moving activity. On the lower astral plane it is desire; on the higher astral plane it is aspiration. On the mental plane it is the urge to search and discover. It is also observation, concentration, analysis, and synthesis. When red mixes with inappropriate colors, and C mixes with inappropriate notes, a tendency to dominate people or a tendency toward cruelty and harshness is created. Red and the note C also have great healing qualities if they are used intelligently and in the right dosage.

C is a destructive note. It destroys limitations, illusions, glamors, and blind urges and drives. Some day people will be able to concentrate the red rays through the mental plane and dissolve tumors, cancerous cells, and atoms in the etheric and physical bodies. Iron, carnelian, garnet, amber, red and green bloodstones, zing plasm, jasper, and ruby radiate red rays and subtones of C.

In the zodiacal signs, Aries and its ruler, Mars, radiate the color red and the note C. Each zodiacal sign has three rulers, which are planets that transmit the energy of the zodiacal sign. The first is the esoteric ruler; the second is the exoteric ruler; the third is the hierarchical ruler. These three planets form a chord for the zodiacal sign, due to their sound waves.

In Aries, the chord is red (C natural), yellow (E natural) and blue-green (G natural). The parts of the body that are affected by this chord and the color red are the head, cerebrospinal system, and the muscular system. Those who are on the red ray are prone to blood ailments, anemia, physical debility and lassitude, colds, circulatory difficulties, and paralysis.

Red is assimilated through the base of the spine center which, when stimulated, causes adrenaline to be released into the bloodstream. Red light helps in the formation of hemoglobin.

The perfume of the red ray is rose or rose oil. The jewel of this ray is the diamond. Red stands for love, courage, adventure, and enthusiasm. Red blended with yellow has a different effect.

Red relates to: balsam of Peru, capsicum, cloves, bromine, iron, red cedar, and musk.

Red-Orange – C#

Red-orange is the note C#. It is related to Taurus, the neck and throat, the thyroid and parathyroid glands, tonsils, atlas, cervical vertebrae, larynx, vocal cords, jaws, carotid arteries, jugular veins, cerebellum, and medulla oblongata. Red-orange has a beneficent effect on these parts of the body, if used intelligently and with the proper dosage and duration.

The keynote of Taurus is devotion, obedience, and patience. Red-orange is very helpful for epilepsy, mental instability, asthma, bronchitis, and rheumatism.

Amber radiates red-orange light. Iron, mother-of-pearl, nickel and pearl, radiate orange light and are very effective for Taurus.

The chord of colors for Taurus is red-orange (C#), yellow-green (F natural), and blue (G).

Orange – D

Orange is the color of Gemini. The note is D natural. Orange stimulates the nerves and nadis, the lungs, arms, and hands. In Asia, those who were exhausted with continual mental work and sleepless nights were wrapped in orange-colored blankets, and the D note was sounded near their beds. This used to change the person's body and lead him to a quick recovery. Orange is related to the heart or to the cardiac ganglion through which the energy of the Sun is circulated in the body.

The chord of this constellation is orange (D natural), green (F#), and blue-violet (A natural). The ruling planet is Mercury.

The metals which radiate orange are iron, calcium, nickel, selenium, zinc, rubidium, manganese, carbon, and oxygen gas.

Orange is the keynote of the physical, emotional, and mental vehicles. Orange, which is a mixture of red and yellow rays, becomes a very potent factor in our physical, emotional, and mental bodies.

The orange ray is the ray of transmutation. It releases fear and annihilates inhibitions. Orange stimulates the pranic triangle through which prana is received and transmuted to the blood through the spleen. It stimulates the flow of adrenaline and has a very powerful influence upon the liver. The liver helps to eliminate toxins from the body.

Orange is the color of Solar Angels, the Lords of Flame. It is also the color of psychic energy in the aura of a person. As the human soul fuses with the Solar

Angel, his aura becomes a flame which radiates orange rays, blended with a white tinge. As the human soul progresses toward the Spiritual Triad, the white flame increases and, together with the orange flame, creates the electromagnetic sphere of man.

Orange predominates in the petals of the causal body.

Orange-Yellow – D#

Orange-yellow is the note D# and is related to Cancer. The parts of the body that are affected by Cancer, the color orange-yellow, or D# are the breasts, stomach, digestive organs, lymphatic glands, esophagus, diaphragm, and liver.

The chord of Cancer is orange-yellow (D#), blue-green (G natural), and violet (A#). This chord can heal certain kinds of depression and inspire joy and enthusiasm, if the music is built upon, or if the colors are arranged in successive waves.

Yellow – E

Yellow and the note E are related to Leo. They are also related to the cerebrum. The pineal gland has a great affinity with the color yellow and the note E. Yellow and E are also related to the shoulders, arms, hands, fingers, lungs, and small intestines.

If yellow is used with the note E and concentrated in the area of the head, it stimulates the brain and helps a person be more discriminative and awake to higher values. It is also known that yellow gives emotional stability and balance. Some mental problems appear when yellow is not used, or when it is unintelligently or improperly mixed with other colors. Excessive yellow causes inertia and depression. An excess in the note E, sometimes heard through electrical instruments, or an inaudible E created through electronic means, creates a very unbalanced mental condition and even complicated sicknesses.

A friend of mine began to feel weaker and weaker from no apparent cause. Visiting his home, I noticed that his refrigerator, which was close to his bedroom, was continuously emanating a mechanical sound on the note E. It was flooding his physical, astral, and mental bodies and leading him into inertia, apathy, and depression.

A wise old man once told me that whenever you feel sick, the first thing to do is to rearrange your bedroom, your home, even your location, if there are no visible causes.

Yellow and the note E affect the thousand-petaled Lotus, or the head center, through the pineal gland, the pituitary body, and the alta major center. Through these glands the physical, emotional, and mental metabolisms are controlled.

Yellow stimulates the liver. Through the action of the liver, it brings purification into the system. It also affects the gallbladder and intestines and helps to eliminate wastes from the body.

The perfume of yellow is jasmine. Yellow is found in copper, brass, silver, ivory, coral, aluminum, zinc, strontium, and cobalt. The elements and gases radiating yellow are carbon, sodium, and phosphorus.

The chord of the sign Leo is yellow (E natural), blue (G#), and red-violet (B natural).

Yellow is the lightest ray in the spectrum, and it cannot be absorbed; it reflects back. It inspires goodness and Intuition.

Yellow-Green – F

The note of yellow-green is F natural. The zodiacal sign is Virgo. The ruling planet is Mercury.

Yellow-green affects the solar plexus, the sympathetic nervous system, the pancreas, the spleen, and most of the digestive system.

The chord for Virgo is yellow-green (F natural), violet (A#), and red (C natural).

Green – F#

Green and the note F# are the color and note of Libra. They are also related to the thyroid and parathyroid glands and to our astral body, emotions, and feelings.

Green is the color of Nature. Together with the note F#, it makes Nature a source of beauty, grace, aspiration, and rhythmic movement. The key of our planet is F#.

When the color green and the corresponding note are in the right proportion in our life, we manifest energy, vigor, and health. Those who feel refreshed in meadows, forests, and mountains need to balance their lives with the color green and its corresponding note.

It is interesting that green also has a strong effect on the kidneys and the lower spine. Some kidney problems can be annihilated with the use of green and by rhythmic sounding of F#. One must be very careful to use the right dosage of this note combined with the color green.

Green has a very soothing effect upon the nervous system. High blood pressure can be normalized by the influence of the color green and the note F#, if the color and the note are combined in a rhythmic sequence. There are many ways to do this. For example, the color green can be shown for one second, then the note sounded for three seconds, or in different rhythms — until one finds the most effective flow of color and sound.

Green and F# can be used to eliminate any un-healthy growth on the skin or in the body. It is even possible to visualize both the color and the note and to focus both energy flows on the area of growths.

A green ray radiates in the spectrum in the wave-length of .00058 millimeters, at the rate of 576 trillion times per second.

The jewels of green are jasper, agate, serpentine, and emerald. The perfume is narcissus.

The chord for green (or balance) is green (F#), vio-let (A#), and red-orange (C#). The note F# is a very powerful note that creates integration with Nature. If it is used in excess, it brings disintegration to form, espe-cially etheric, emotional, and mental forms, and disintegration proceeds to the objective form. People must be very careful not be exposed to any mechanical sound equal to F#.

Blue-Green – G

Blue-green and the note G natural are related to Scorpio. The ruler is Mars.

Blue-green is related to the nose, generative system, bladder, urethra, prostate gland, large intestine, and colon. When the chord is organized intelligently, it brings great revitalization to the corresponding areas of the body. The chord of Scorpio is blue-green (G natural), red-violet (B natural), and orange (D natural).

When this chord is used in the right dosage and right duration, it will create transmutation in the astral realms, expansion on the mental plane, and creativity in the spirit of man.

Blue – G#

Blue is related to the note G# and to the constellation Sagittarius. The ruler is Jupiter. Blue is directly connected to the pituitary body, and through it the center between the eyebrows — the ajna center. The pituitary body regulates the rhythm of all systems in the body. Sages have suggested that women in their menstrual cycle wear the color blue and listen to music based upon G#. Overall, this also helps the lymphatic and glandular systems.

Blue and its corresponding note also affect the stomach and breasts, especially in women. In some cases, the ovaries and testes are influenced by blue. In one of the monasteries where I studied, a very old Teacher used to take adolescent children, those in puberty, to the mountains and make them lie down on their backs to watch the blue sky for twenty minutes. When I asked him the reason for this exercise, he answered that blue regulates the cycles, invigorates and heals the testes and ovaries, and helps the breasts to grow in the right proportion. I remember watching the sky as he would play the flute. I would guess that he used to combine the blue of the sky with music based on the note G#. We used to feel extremely invigorated, energetic, and joyful after this twenty-minute exercise of gazing at the blue sky and listening to his music.

The chord of Sagittarius is blue (G#), red (C natural), and yellow-orange (D#). When arranged intelligently, these colors and notes can inspire unity, worship, and foresight.

Blue is found in copper, opal, nickel, topaz, moonstone, aquamarine, blue-lace agate, and so on. The blue ray is very antiseptic. Places where the walls, carpeting, or curtains are blue reject those who come with polluted intention; they feel like leaving and they go away. It also repels thoughtforms which carry psychological germs.

The blue ray is very healing and soothing for bleeding, irritation, apoplexy, hysteria, epilepsy, cholera, measles, the thyroid, and so on.

In a monastery where I studied, the Teachers used to let us watch the sky before going to bed. The blue sky gave us a deep sense of sleep in which our memory of events was very vivid. Blue inspires the mood of meditation, devotion, mystic aspiration, and intuitive awareness.

The blue ray supplies oxygen to the body and fiery vitality to thought. The wavelength of this ray vibrates at 653 trillion times per second.

Blue-Violet – A

Blue-violet is related to the note A natural and to Capricorn. The ruler is Saturn. Blue-violet, Capricorn, and A natural are related to the knees, skin, and sweat glands. They are also related to the sacral center, kidneys, and bones.

The chord is blue-violet (A natural), red (C natural), and orange-yellow (D#). Such a combination, especially when the Sun is in Capricorn, brings great regeneration to the above-mentioned parts of the body.

Violet – A#

Violet (or purple) and the note A# are related to the sign of Aquarius. The ruler is Uranus. The chord is violet (A#), orange (D natural), and yellow-green (F natural).

Violet is very effective for the knees, ankles, and nervous system. If the chord is used intelligently, great relief will be felt in these areas and the person will be inspired with humility, brotherhood, and aspiration toward perfection.

Violet is found in iron, platinum, sapphire, amethyst, and onyx.

Red-Violet – B

Red-violet and the note B are related to the constellation of Pisces. The ruler is Jupiter. The chord is red-violet (B natural), yellow-orange (D#), and green (F#).

Red-violet and the note B affect the feet, toes, and skin. If the chord is used intelligently and in the right dosage and duration, many problems of the feet, toes, and skin can be solved and the subject will be inspired by the virtues of fidelity, hospitality, and understanding.

Chapter 14

The Senses of the Sun

The senses of the Sun are its Seven Rays.

- The Seventh Ray is its hearing — indigo.
- The Sixth Ray is its taste — violet.
- The Fifth Ray is its intellect — green.
- The Fourth Ray is its smell — orange.
- The Third Ray is its sight — yellow.
- The Second Ray is its intuition — blue.
- The First Ray is its touch — red.

Uniformity of color was imposed in certain activities. For example, in certain groups, people would wear blue or red. This imposition was established to maintain harmony between the members and the goals of the group. But then this changed, and people now feel free to dress in any color they want. If they dress in colors that do not harmonize with the group and its goal, the group shows signs of disintegration.

It is possible to dress in different colors if those colors are in harmony, or if the fusion or mixture of color creates a color which is the goals of the group. Thus, one person can bring disharmony by wearing a color that does not fit the general tone of color.

The same phenomenon can be seen in decorations, paintings, flower arrangements, and in dance costumes. Color is like music; it must express harmony and rhythm.

Movements Related with Zodiacal Signs

Aries	always straight lines
Taurus	curved movement; neck movement
Gemini	parallel movement; arm, shoulder and hand movements
Cancer	round movement; belly movement
Leo	circle movement; chest movement
Virgo	swinging movement; lower torso
Libra	contrasting movement; lower torso, triangular or half circle
Scorpio	forward, backward, right and left movement; lower belly
Sagittarius	running steps; thigh movement
Capricorn	jumping movement; knee movement
Aquarius	sliding movement; ankle movement
Pisces	lifting movement; feet movement

Planets and Correspondences

Neptune	spinal fluid, pineal gland
Uranus	pituitary
Mercury	thymus
Venus	thyroid
Sun	spleen, pons Varolii
Jupiter	two adrenals
Mars	left cerebrum, motor nerve, spinal cord
Mercury	right cerebrum, sensory nerve, spinal cord
Moon	sympathetic nerves, spinal cord

In the art of painting, **Aries** is symbolized with straight lines by steep mountains, precipices, rivers, trees, swords, and so on, with a suggestion of striving using the color red.

Taurus is symbolized with curvy lines or half circles. Its virtue is gratitude, the spirit of thankfulness, which can be represented by an element in Nature, for example, a bull in a field, a deer by a river, a bird in a tree, a blooming tree with a blue sky, a girl in admiration.

A Taurus painting must radiate gratitude and admiration, and the artist must find a subtle way to present it. The predominating color is red-orange.

Gemini is symbolized by parallel lines, curved or straight. In the painting there must be parallelism, mostly indicated by the use of the color orange. Thus, the parallelism must be mathematically accurate in the lines of buildings, rivers, roads, bridges, clouds, reflections. The dominating color must be that color which creates the parallels. The spirit is harmlessness.

Cancer is symbolized by circular lines, such as flowers, planets, fruit, faces, plates, disks, and so on. The predominating color should be yellow-orange. The spirit is discrimination. The artist must create those events or relationships in a painting which subtly suggest the spirit of discrimination.

Leo is symbolized by a round spiral formation in rocks, bushes, trees, animals, clouds, and so on, but they must be scattered in different places in the painting with the color yellow.

The viewer must unconsciously register the formation of the yellow as a round spiral. For example, the yellow color on different objects, when joined in a proper way, will form a round spiral. The spirit is courage.

Virgo is symbolized by wavy lines, swinging movements. The spirit is solemnity, and the predominating color is yellow-green.

Libra is symbolized by contrasting triangular or half circular lines. The dominating color is green. The spirit is responsibility.

Scorpio is symbolized by lines or forms that move forward and backward, similar to zigzags, but always advancing toward Infinity. The predominating color is blue-green. The spirit is fearlessness. The artist must charge the formation with the spirit of fearlessness.

Sagittarius is symbolized by climbing lines, like a path circling around a mountain, partly visible, partly invisible. The predominating color will be blue. The spirit is patience, balance, rest, and peace, with an accumulating power of possible conclusion. It must suggest successive goals to be achieved.

Capricorn is symbolized by jumping lines or dotted lines that have continuity but breaks in them as well. The form or line must be unexpected. The jumping line should be forward-moving but not straight. It is a mixture of curved and straight lines, with blue-violet predominating and a spirit of daring.

Aquarius is symbolized by harmony of lines, forms, shapes, and colors in the painting. The painting is predominantly violet in color. The spirit is compassion and inclusiveness. Aquarius can be symbolized by rivers, doors, windows, arches, givingness, abundance, and opportunity.

Pisces is symbolized by lifting lines. The predominating color is red-violet. The spirit is service.

People have the idea that virtues are human qualities, but virtues belong to any form of life and to all kingdoms. A talented artist can radiate the spirit upon the whole painting with a symbol which serves as the connecting and focusing link for the rest.

The proportion of the intensity of the color to the size of the symbol or form is important. The brighter, stronger, and purer the color, the larger the symbol should be, as its size can transmit the intensity focused in the painting. The fainter and more vague the color, the smaller the symbol must be to condense the focus of the impression of the color. It is not necessary to show the symbol in its actual lines, but it must contain subliminal, subjective construction through the invisible lines connected with key points on the painting. True art objects are not seen by the intellect but by the Intuition. Intuition does not like to be trapped in geometrical forms.

The zodiacal signs are divided into three groups, each of which has four signs. These three groups are

— Cardinal   Aries, Cancer, Libra, Capricorn
— Fixed   Taurus, Leo, Scorpio, Aquarius
— Mutable   Gemini, Virgo, Sagittarius, Pisces

The painting can have the predominating color and line formation of Aries, Taurus, or Gemini; or if mixed, the painting must have colors, notes, and movements of the individual crosses if harmony and impression are going to be maintained. For example, if one is creating music or painting on Aries, complimentary notes and colors which relate to Cancer, Libra, and Capricorn must be used.

Remember that there are three primary colors: red, yellow, and blue. Orange, green, violet, and indigo are mixtures. The hues of these colors are twelve, just as there are twelve notes in the chromatic scale.

The musician of color will use color to create his painting, just as a musician of sound creates his symphony with notes.

Chapter 15

Shock Absorbers

Nature has a system of shock absorbers, protective electromagnetic walls which enable all forms to advance in an orderly manner in spite of local disturbances, explosions, Cosmic electrical storms, or a sudden rush or flow of energies in space or in any form. It is these shock absorbers or protective walls that provide conditions of survival for the many forms on the path of evolution.

In the human constitution, there are many shock absorbers in the physical, emotional, and mental realms. On the physical plane, muscles and nerves have their shock-absorbing function and mechanism. The senses are also equipped with such mechanisms.

The etheric body has its own shock-absorbing system which balances the inflow of energies presented in

many forms. These are the etheric centers and their petals.

In the emotional body we have the mechanism of
imagination, which works in a very mysterious manner
to absorb various shocks and keep us going forward on
the path of our life.

In the mental body we have beliefs, religion, tradition, thoughts, and ideas, which build a shock-absorbing
mechanism if they are handled correctly. Creative imagination and visualization are also powerful shock-absorbing mechanisms.

In the emotional and mental bodies we have higher
correspondences of etheric centers and their petals, which
form a sophisticated shock-absorbing mechanism. The
twelve-petaled Lotus is a great shock-absorbing mechanism which also protects the developing human soul from
subtle psychic attacks and planetary and solar pressures
caused by great explosions, solar winds and storms, or
mobilized destructive actions of the dark forces. Similar
correspondences exist for the planet, for the solar system, and for the galaxy.

In our planet, humanity as a whole is a great shock
absorber for the lower kingdoms. The planetary Hierarchy is a great shock-absorber and protective wall for
humanity and the lower kingdoms.

"The center where the Will of God is known" is
another great shock-absorbing mechanism which protects
the Hierarchy and Initiates from solar attacks and storms
and from the pressures of certain active energies in the
Cosmos.

It should be known that the same correspondences exist in higher and higher planes and in higher forms. Thus, the whole Cosmos is engineered in such a manner that the destructive work does not interfere with the constructive work carried out on all planes.

On the human level and on all other levels, it is possible that the "entity" weakens his protective net or the shock-absorbing mechanism, thus prematurely inviting destructive forces to carry out a process of disintegration within his vehicles. The protective net and shock-absorbing mechanisms can be sustained in a healthy condition only by keeping in tune with the *direction* of the Cosmic Magnet. All great religions and their source, the Teaching, provide the techniques to find the Direction of the Cosmic Magnet.

The aura of the man, the atmosphere around the globe, and the solar radiation in the body of the solar system are also protective nets. These protective nets are damaged by human thoughts if they are not in tune with the Law of Compassion. The negative and destructive human thoughts as a whole, and the pollution coming from the surface of this planet, damage and weaken the protective planetary net of the atmosphere. The solar protective network is damaged by the collective vibrations emanating from each planet and moon in the solar system.

It is also evident that these protective nets are strengthened and highly organized by individual thoughts or by thoughts of humanity as a whole regarding Beauty, Goodness, and Truth. These repair and renew the damaged parts of the protective net. Planetary networks are repaired by the emanations and spiritual labor of great Teachers and the Hierarchy. The solar network is strengthened by certain comets and extra-planetary Beings.

Thus, in the whole Cosmos we find the hand of the Great Ones protecting and leading the children on the path of Infinite development.

Chapter 16

Deposits

People always need a proper place for their refuse, for their physical waste and trash. And they create various systems to solve the problem of waste disposal through sewage and septic systems, trash collection, and special places to dump their trash.

Just as the physical body has its sewage system and dump yards, the same is true for the emotional and mental bodies, which have a similar need to rid themselves of their trash. All wastes in the emotional and mental bodies are accumulated in the aura, the magnetic container of the person.

This collection of trash is packaged by the clean parts of the body and isolated from the rest of the aura. We have emotions which our system digests and uses as nourishment. There are those emotions, however, that we cannot digest or assimilate. All negative emotions pass through our emotional digestive system and collect themselves in the appropriately-constructed receptacle in the aura. In the meantime, they damage the digestive system, if they are poisonous or contaminated with hatred, murder, or treason.

We have thoughts which nourish our mental body, but we also have thoughts which cannot be assimilated by our system. There are thoughts which are related to vanity, ego, separatism, illusion, and so on. These thoughts are undigestible elements which pass through our system, often damaging it, and collect themselves in the mental dump yard or trash can.

At the time of a negative mood, some people go and dig into these trash cans and use their contents against others, or even against themselves. These trash cans within the aura give us a very uncomfortable feeling, anxiety, fear, depression, and so on. In their presence, the vitality of the etheric body, the aspiration of the emotional body, the striving of the mental body, slowly weaken and sometimes even totally disappear; then the human soul becomes a victim of inertia, apathy, and depression.

For the sake of health, sanity, and joy, a person must try first, to clean the trash from his aura, and then second, never collect trash again. Unfortunately it is not possible to dump or cleanse the collected trash outside of the aura.

The cleansing process is formulated as follows:

1. Observation and realization that trash exists within you
2. Awareness of the nature of the trash
3. Making sure not to increase the trash
4. Taking action to eliminate the trash

In order to eliminate emotional trash, one can daily increase his gratitude, love, joy, respectfulness, inclusiveness, and desirelessness and try to conquer hatred, fear, anger, jealousy, revenge, slander, malice, and treason.

In regard to mental trash, striving toward perfection, trying to improve oneself month after month, trying to see the illusions, and attempting to think clearly all help to eliminate the trash.

After taking such steps, a person will notice that his positive emotions and clear thinking will slowly consume the contents of the trash cans in his aura and use these contents as fertilizer for new growth and expansion.

Our health and happiness disappear when our aura turns into a dump yard. **Meditation, evening review, sacrificial service**, and **aspiration** are four major cleansing processes.

Meditation naturally draws out the contents of the trash cans and burns them. One does not meditate on the trash but penetrates through meditation and then charges the aura with heavenly fire. The fire generated by contact with higher spheres through meditation serves to burn the trash. It is only after the trash is gone that one can enjoy freedom and joy.

Evening review creates a strong warning or alarm system in the mental body. When the trash is cast out into the aura, the person is cautioned or warned.

Sacrificial service brings higher currents of energy from our Core. Such currents are very destructive to trash that has been accumulated throughout ages.

Aspiration is a form of striving toward a vision which is actualized by steady devotion and dedication. The fire of aspiration disintegrates glamor and emotional trash and cleanses the mirror of Intuition.

The average aura is full of trash; it is this trash which primarily affects the organs in the body by exercising varying degrees of pressure, and it also serves as a hotbed of germs and viruses.

A purified aura is the shield of the body, heart, and brain. A purified aura resembles a beautiful flower, a rainbow through which vital energies circulate, spreading happiness, joy, and bliss.

Index

About the Author

Torkom Saraydarian (1917 – 1997) was born in Asia Minor. Since childhood he was trained in the Teachings of the Ageless Wisdom under the guidance of his loving father.

As he grew up, he visited monasteries, ancient temples, and mystery schools in order to find the answers to his questions about the mystery of man and the Universe. He studied with Sufis, dervishes, Christian mystics, and masters of temple music and dance.

He was musically trained and was able to play the violin, piano, oud, cello, and guitar. He composed hundreds of musical pieces that embody his training and striving.

Torkom Saraydarian dedicated his entire life to the service of his fellow man. His writings and lectures and music show his total devotion to the higher principles, values, and laws that are present in all world religions and philosophies. These works represent a synthesis of the best and most beautiful in the sacred culture of the world. His works enrich the foundational thinking on which man can construct his Future.

Torkom Saraydarian wrote a large number of books, many of which have been published. All of his books will continue to be published and distributed. Many have been translated into Armenian, German, Italian, Spanish, Portuguese, Greek, Dutch, and Danish.

He left a rich legacy of writings and musical compositions for all of humanity to enjoy and benefit from for many years to come.

Other Books by Torkom Saraydarian

- The Ageless Wisdom
- The Aura
- Battling Dark Forces
- The Bhagavad Gita
- Breakthrough to Higher Psychism
- Buddha Sutra — A Dialogue with the Glorious One
- Challenge for Discipleship
- Christ, The Avatar of Sacrificial Love
- A Commentary on Psychic Energy
- Cosmic Shocks
- Cosmos in Man
- The Creative Fire
- Dynamics of Success
- Educating the Whole Person, Vol. I
- Educating the Whole Person, Vol. II
- The Eyes of Hierarchy — How the Masters Watch and Help Us
- Flame of Beauty, Culture, Love, Joy
- The Flame of the Heart
- From My Heart — Volume I (Poetry)
- Hiawatha and the Great Peace
- The Hidden Glory of the Inner Man
- I Was
- Joy and Healing
- Leadership Vol. I
- Leadership Vol. II
- Leadership Vol. III
- Leadership Vol. IV
- Leadership Vol. V
- Legend of Shamballa
- The Mystery of Self-Image
- The Mysteries of Willpower
- New Dimensions in Healing
- Olympus World Report...The Year 3000
- One Hundred Names of God
- Other Worlds
- The Psyche and Psychism
- The Psychology of Cooperation and Group Consciousness
- The Purpose of Life
- The Science of Becoming Oneself
- The Science of Meditation
- The Sense of Responsibility in Society
- Sex, Family, and the Woman in Society
- The Solar Angel
- Spiritual Regeneration
- Spring of Prosperity
- The Subconscious Mind and the Chalice
- Symphony of the Zodiac
- Talks on Agni
- Teaching the Ageless Wisdom
- Thought and the Glory of Thinking
- Triangles of Fire
- Unusual Court
- Woman, Torch of the Future
- The Year 2000 & After

Booklets

- The Art of Visualization —
  Simply Presented
- The Chalice in Agni Yoga
  Literature
- Cornerstones of Health
- A Daily Discipline of Worship
- Discipleship in Action
- Duties of Grandparents
- Earrings for Business People
- Earthquakes and Disasters —
  What the Ageless Wisdom
  Tells Us
- Fiery Carriage and Drugs
- Five Great Mantrams of the
  New Age
- Hierarchy and the Plan
- How to Find Your Level of
  Meditation
- Inner Blooming
- Irritation — The Destructive
  Fire
- Mental Exercises
- Nachiketas
- New Beginnings
- Practical Spirituality
- Questioning Traveler and Karma
- Saint Sergius

- Synthesis

Booklets
(Excerpts and Compilations)

- Angels and Devas
- Building Family Unity
- Courage
- Daily Spiritual Striving
- First Steps Toward Freedom
- Prayers, Mantrams, and Invoca-
  tions
- The Psychology of Cooperation
- Responsibility
- Responsibility and Business
- Responsibilities of Fathers
- Responsibilities of Mothers
- Success
- Torchbearers
- What to Look for in the Heart
  of Your Partner

Videos

- The Seven Rays Interpreted
- Why Drugs Are Dangerous
*(Lecture videos available on
  hundreds of topics, both in
  stock and by special order.
  Call us for details.)*

We are continuously adding new releases.
For an updated list of publications, please
contact T.S.G. Publishing Foundation, Inc.

Visit our web-site at www.tsg-publishing.com.

About the Publisher

T.S.G. Publishing Foundation, Inc. is a non-profit, tax exempt organization. Founded on November 30, 1987 in Los Angles, California, it relocated to Cave Creek, Arizona on January 1, 1994.

Our purpose is to be a pathway for self-transformation. We are fully devoted to publishing, teaching, and distributing the creative works of Torkom Saraydarian.

Our bookstore in Cave Creek and our online bookstore at our web site *www.tsg-publishing.com* offer the complete collection of the creative works of Torkom Saraydarian for sale and distribution. Our newsletter OUTREACH contains thought-provoking articles excerpted from these books. We also conduct weekly classes, special training seminars, and home study meditation courses.

Please contact us or visit our web site *www.tsg-publishing.com* if you wish to have additional information about our organization and our activities.

Torkom Saraydarian
Book Publishing Fund

Torkom Saraydarian dedicated his entire life to serving others in their spiritual growth. At the time of his passing, more than 100 manuscripts had been written and prepared for publication. This work represents a seamless tapestry of Wisdom and we are dedicated to publishing the entire collection.

Torkom Saraydarian had the unique wisdom and dedication to write all of these magnificent books in one lifetime. Now it is our turn to do the work. Together we can make his dream a reality and bring his legacy to fruition.

We depend on contributions for the publishing of the books. A special fund, *The Torkom Saraydarian Book Publishing Fund* has been established for the completion of this legacy. Contact us for details about the *Book Fund* and an update regarding remaining manuscripts. You can contribute funds for an entire book, or give any amount you wish on a continuous basis or a one-time contribution.

Your contributions will entitle you to devote an entire book to a loved one, or share the dedication with others in the *Book Fund*.

Thank you for your loving and continuous support.

Ordering Information

Write to the publisher for additional information regarding:
— Free catalog of author's books and music tapes
— Complete list of lecture tapes and videos
  ($2 postage for each list)
— Placement on mailing list for continuous updates
— A free copy of our newsletter *Outreach*
— **Join our Book Club at no charge. (Receive a 20% discount with each new release by Torkom Saraydarian. Each new book is mailed to you automatically as soon as it is released.) Send us a written approval to include you in the Book Club.**

Additional copies of *The Aura*
U.S. $15.00

Postage within U.S.A. – $5.00 plus applicable state sales tax
International postage: contact us for surface or air rates.

T.S.G. Publishing Foundation, Inc.
P.O. Box 7068
Cave Creek, AZ 85327–7068
United States of America
TEL: (480) 502–1909
FAX: (480) 502–0713
E-Mail: webmaster@tsg-publishing.com
Web-site: www.tsg-publishing.com

Participate in the Vision for the Future

Contribute to
The Torkom Saraydarian
Book Publishing Fund

My Pledge:

❖ ❑ One-time: $ _____ ❑ Annually: $ _____ ❑ Monthly: $ _____ ❖

Name: _____

Address: _____

City / State: _____ Country: _____

Tel #: (___) _____ –

E-mail Address: _____

Method of Payment: ❑ Check/U.S. Money-order   ❑ Visa   ❑ MasterCard

Account # _____ – _____ – _____   Exp. date: ___ /

(If using credit card, please include account number & expiration date)

Please send to:

**T.S.G. Publishing Foundation, Inc. • Attn: Book Fund
P.O. Box 7068 • Cave Creek, AZ 85327 • U.S.A.
Tel: (480) 502-1909 • Fax: (480) 502-0713**

Web site: *www.tsg-publishing.com*
E-mail: *webmaster@tsg-publishing.com*

T.S.G. Publishing Foundation, Inc. is a tax-exempt, non-profit organization.

❑ I would like to pay for the publishing of a book in its entirely. (Please tell us what you want on the dedication page.)

❑ Please include my name on the list of donors.

❑ No name please, just add this donation to the Book Fund.